Fashioning a People Today

The Educational Insights of Maria Harris

GABRIEL MORAN

FASHIONING
A PEOPLE
TODAY

THE EDUCATIONAL INSIGHTS
OF MARIA HARRIS

Twenty-Third Publications
A Division of Bayard
One Montauk Avenue, Suite 200
New London, CT 06320
(860) 437-3012 or (800) 321-0411
www.23rdpublications.com

ISBN 978-1-58595-605-0
Library of Congress Catalog Card Number: 2006927961
Printed in the U.S.A.

Contents

Introduction

"In the beginning is relation," wrote Martin Buber. We live in the present when we are present to other living and speaking beings. Within that present the past is to be found, a past that is not disappearing behind our backs but is forming another layer of the ground we stand on. This view of time, not as a series of points but as presence, means that dialogue includes those who have gone before us and still speak to us.

We rightly say, in referring to the *Republic*, that Plato says...or that Thomas Aquinas says in the *Summa*...or that Martin Buber says.... They remain interlocutors in our community of discourse. Gorky once said of Tolstoy, "So long as that man is alive, I am not alone in the world." I have often wondered what Gorky had to say after 1916 when Tolstoy died, twenty years before Gorky did. What I suspect is that Gorky altered his worldview to the extent that, although Tolstoy had indeed died, his words could continue to sustain Gorky and hundreds of thousands of other people. As C.S. Lewis found while grieving the death of his friend Charles Williams, "When my idea of death met my idea of Williams, it was my idea of death that changed."

In a book written some years ago, Andrew Greeley reported on people who claimed to be in contact with the dead. Greeley drew from an NORC survey with findings that forty-two percent of people admitted to conversing with the dead. Some people might think that this practice among such a large slice of the population is a sign of widespread insanity. I think, on the contrary, it is what keeps the human race sane by not losing contact with the mind and words of those we cherish.

This reflection on presence and dialogue sets the context for understanding the somewhat peculiar nature of this book. For me, this book flows naturally from my daily conversations. For the reader, however, the book might seem strange and awkward, even a little spooky. This book is a conversation with church thinkers, past and present, about education. It is also a conversation with secular educators about what they might both teach the church and learn from the church. More directly, however, this book is a conversation with one person who died in 2005: Maria Harris. Maria and I conversed about everything for thirty-nine years until her voice was stilled by death. At that point, the dialogue radically shifted but it did not disappear. When I write throughout this book that "Maria says," this is more than a figure of speech for me.

This book, to be even more precise, is a dialogue with one of Maria's books, *Fashion Me a People*. At the time she wrote it, she thought of it as a modest contribution to discussions of church curriculum, but the book has been a mainstay for Protestant and Catholic educators. I have no desire to write a substitute book or to offer corrections of her book. Good books speak to the moment and they are also timeless. Some references become dated but the insightful author touches chords that allow perceptive readers to fill in their own references.

Why then this book? I offer reflections that are my own but are inspired and guided by the framework of *Fashion Me a People*. As one of the perceptive readers of the book, I am simply adding my voice to a continuing conversation about church curriculum. As someone who was there for the writing of every sentence in *Fashion Me a People*, I might be able to provide a context for other readers and draw out what the book says for today.

I recognize that such an undertaking is presumptuous, but every book, especially in philosophy and religion, is a commentary on preceding books. That fact can produce arrogance. When Martin Heidegger was criticized for his interpretation of Immanuel Kant, his defense was: I know Kant better than Kant does. Maybe Heidegger writing on Kant can get away with such a claim; after all, there is a sense in which the meaning of Kant is clearer in Heidegger's twentieth century than it could be to Kant himself. In that sense, Aquinas was a better Aristotelian than Aristotle; Whitehead is a better Platonist than Plato. Most of us have to be less presumptuous, writing our commentaries on a range of writers within a philosophical or religious tradition, while aware of our limitations in trying to understand any particular writer.

The aim of this book is very limited: a conversation with the author of *Fashion Me a People*. The project is still ambitious if not arrogant, and I would not attempt it with any other author. The reader may still be suspicious that I am exploiting the work of another author. My final defense comes down to one unshakable conviction, namely that Maria would enthusiastically endorse this project. Anyone who knew Maria will know what I mean by invoking her enthusiasm.

For the reader who is unacquainted with *Fashion Me a People*, I think my reflections in this book can stand on their own and be of some value. However, the reader of Maria's book is likely to find this book more intelligible and practical, having access to both sides of the conversation. I would consider it a worthy accomplishment of this book if it leads to more readers for *Fashion Me a People*. Readers who personally knew Maria will, I hope, be able to inject into these pages some of the liveliness, compassion, and artistry that flowed from Maria's personality and infused everything she did.

The plan of this book is a simple one, very simple for readers of *Fashion Me a People*. I will follow the outline of Maria's book with only a few changes. I begin with a chapter on the church's mission, both religious and educational. I then discuss the idea of curriculum as a lifelong and life wide learning experience. After that, I proceed to consider in turn each of the five curricular forms that Maria identified from the Acts of the Apostle 2:42–47: community, liturgy, proclamation, teaching, and service.

In each of these chapters, I begin with a passage from *Fashion Me a People*. These quotations are chosen for inspiration and guidance rather than exegesis. Within each chapter, I make further references to Maria's book and I occasionally bring in other writings of hers as the conversation suggests. In a conversation between people who have known each other for a long time, much of the conversation is in what is unsaid or what is conveyed by a passing phrase that sets off a chain of memories. I invite the reader to join in the jostling of my own memory of what has happened during the past forty years with the church and its education. All of my memories are inextricably bound with Maria Harris and the great encouragement she gave to educators in the church and beyond.

Where this book departs from the format of *Fashion Me a People* is in its beginning and its end. I have created bookends in the form of an Introduction and an Epilogue. The seven chapters that parallel *Fashion Me a People* are embraced by a memoir about Maria Harris. What follows in this Introduction is a brief narrative of her life and work. At the other end of this book, the Epilogue is a longer story of her sickness and death. The material in both of these bookends is from a memoir that I wrote after her death.

At the time of Maria's funeral, many people asked me whether I planned to write something about her illness and death. I said that I was not inclined to do so. My reticence came from two sources. For her part, I thought that the four years of her illness was a private matter. There are many details of a person's grave illness that need not go beyond a hospital chart or a psychiatrist's notes. For my part, I had no idea how to write a memoir, one that would honor her memory and protect the privacy due even after her death.

Nine months later, I changed my mind. I am glad I did so then. Six months earlier would have been too soon to unlock some memories and six months later would have been too late for retaining the freshness of some memories. The shift in my thinking about writing was influenced by the course on death that I was teaching to forty undergraduates at NYU. The students were very understanding. I had given them a warning in the first class. I said that in my forty-nine years of classroom teaching, I had never had the problem of breaking into tears, but it might happen in this course.

During the course, I had lunch with a hospice nurse who had been coming to the class for ten years; the conversation with her was the tipping point. I immediately decided to write something. I was unsure of what I would write, how to design it, or how long it would be. I simply aimed to put on paper the memories bouncing around in my head. Once I began to write, the material flowed effortlessly and I completed the work almost nonstop.

I described what I wrote in an extended letter to Maria's friends. I sent the piece to about 150 people who I thought would understand my intention. I said then that I had no desire to publish it for a larger audience. I found, however, that many of the people who received the essay passed it on to friends. I was not unhappy about such sharing of the material and I did not try to restrict the circulation. But I am altering my original intention by publishing most of this memoir here. I have removed some of the private details but for the most part I have left unedited what I wrote in November of 2005.

I think this book is an appropriate context for sharing the essay with a wider reading public. The logic of religion is much closer to the aesthetic experience than to the scientific. The truth of religion is reached not by replicating experiments or abstracting concepts from individual cases, but by reflecting deeply on a single work of art or the lives of a small group of people. Christianity even has the audacity to claim that history can be revealed in the life, death, and resurrection of one person (situated in his community).

The paradox of religion is captured in the contrasting meanings of "unique." Unique means different from all others. The difference can be exclusive or inclusive. The specifically human form of uniqueness is a differing from others by a process of increasing inclusiveness. It is precisely because each human life is unique that it can be revelatory to every other person. I write about Maria's experience as uniquely her experience, which means that anyone who is open to reflecting upon it can find something revealed about his or her own life. The narrative of Maria's death is thus the exemplar of the logic in this book.

I was particularly inspired by an essay published in *Cross Currents* at the time that Maria was diagnosed with dementia. Gisela Webb, a professor of religious studies, wrote about her experience with her mother who suffered from Alzheimer's for sixteen years. The essay, "Intimations of the Great Unknowing: Interreligious Spirituality and the Demise of Consciousness Which is Alzheimer's," documents one woman's experience aided by reflection drawn from Buddhist and Muslim as well as Christian religions. I wrote to the author to tell her that in all my searching through literature on dementia, I had found her essay to be the most theoretically profound and also the most practically helpful. In fact, it was the only piece of writing that gave me any religious meaning to hold on to amid the horror of watching the decline into dementia.

My experience with Maria was unique, and therefore of potential interest to the twenty-eight million people in the country who are currently coping with the dementia of a family member. Here, then, in the remainder of this introduction is a brief background about Maria's life and writing, including the book *Fashion Me a People*. Later, in the Epilogue, if the reader wishes to pursue the story, they can read the account of Maria's illness and death.

Maria's Story

Maria Harris, having grown up in Queens and Brooklyn, was a loyal New Yorker. For many years, she studied music and taught in elementary schools, a background that later made her such a good teacher in the seminary and university. She had gone to St. John's University for one year before entering the Sisters of Saint Joseph of Brentwood, Long Island. As was not unusual at the time, it took her sixteen summers to earn her B.A. After that, her academic career moved quickly. She received a master's degree in catechetical theology at Manhattan College in 1967. Then she went straight for her doctorate in 1972 from the joint program at Teachers College Columbia and Union Theological Seminary. Her most important teacher at Union was Mary Tully who taught art and quickly recognized Maria as a protégé.

While studying for her degree, Maria began work in the diocesan office of Rockville Center with Frederick Schaefer, who besides being her boss became a great friend. She was appointed to work with the emerging group of people known as parish directors of religious education. In fact, she wrote *The DRE Book*, which helped establish the field and give a name to the role. Very quickly, she was in demand across the country, and for the rest of her life, educators in Catholic parishes held her in high regard.

Her next move broadened the base of those who looked to her for support. In 1975, she became a professor at Andover Newton Theological School, a seminary outside of Boston. I was skeptical, wanting to know how an Irish Catholic girl from Brooklyn could possibly fit in with New England Baptists and Congregationalists. To my surprise—though I should have known better—she immediately became good friends with faculty members and became one of the most popular teachers in the school as well.

After a few years she was appointed to the Howard Chair of Religious Education. At her installation, I was one of several speakers (representing the Catholic Church). I reflected on the fact that Maria was the first Roman Catholic faculty member of the school. And it was a school founded in 1807 "to counteract the influence of Unitarians, atheists, and papists." I said that perhaps the founders of Andover Seminary were rolling over in their graves, but I suspected they would recognize that her presence only brought to the school vitality, intelligence, and a profound religious sensibility. That this indeed proved to be the case was evidenced at the time of her death by numerous written testimonies from faculty and former students on the school's Web site.

Maria left the place where she was respected and loved only because she missed New York. She thought that she would like to teach for a semester each year and freelance for the other semester. By this time, she was in demand as much from Protestant audiences as Catholic, and she liked traveling to places around the United States and beyond. Not knowing if such an arrangement was a realistic possibility, she consulted with Vincent Novak who headed the Fordham program where she had taught as an adjunct professor before going to Andover Newton. When Father Novak heard what she was looking for, his response was: Why not come to Fordham and do that? She was surprised at being able to arrange the deal so easily, but Fordham knew that the luck was on their side.

Maria taught at Fordham for a semester each year until she decided to be self-employed in the mid-1990s. She had more than enough to keep her busy. I did not fully appreciate how hard she worked until I went through her papers after she died. Most people who are regularly invited to speak on a few themes have a stock speech to which they give some local coloring. But what I found in Maria's materials was that she prepared each weekend workshop in meticulous detail, both the content of what she would say and how she would present it. She was a very engaging speaker from a lecture platform and she was even better in a classroom with a small group of students.

Maria always thought of herself as a writer by accident. She never set out to be an author of books. Her first books simply came along as an accompaniment to her teaching. I think the book *Fashion Me a People* in 1989 was a breakthrough for her in her self-image as an author. Craig Dykstra, who at that time was at Princeton Seminary, gave her a lot of help in preparing that text, and she got a better sense of what an author is. The book is still selling well, being used as a curriculum guide in Protestant seminaries and Catholic programs of religious education.

When a literary agent pushed Maria to write a book on women and spirituality, she dashed off an outline whose main purpose was getting rid of the agent. The agent went to Bantam Press and got a huge advance based on the outline. Writing *Dance of the Spirit* was perhaps the most difficult writing project she ever undertook. The result was a beautiful work that fully satisfied the Bantam editors and the book sold well. That experience led to a second book with Bantam. When Maria first proposed a book on older women and spirituality, Bantam was skeptical but she eventually persuaded them. This time Maria negotiated her own contract. After writing the book *Jubilee Time* for Bantam, she had some additional material that she thought might be made into a book for a church readership. She quickly put together a small volume, *Proclaim Jubilee!*

This book took note of the coming year 2000, which was about five years in the future. The year 2000 was a jubilee year in which debts were to be forgiven. During the years leading up to the new millennium, she became a strong voice in the movement to forgive the debts of poor nations that were burdened with impossible interest payments. The New York newspaper *Newsday* did a Sunday feature on Maria's work in this area. She was invited to numerous parishes to speak on what individuals and parishes could do for the jubilee year.

She had two other themes that interested her and drew invitations. She was invited to speak to many women's groups and to wrestle with the issues of the feminist movement. She was especially interested in the development of young girls, and often spoke to women faculty of high schools and colleges. A further issue dear to her heart was Jewish-Christian relations. She often worked with the *Facing History* curriculum that deals with twentieth-century genocide. She became deeply committed to the appreciation of the Jewish people and their history. We once attended a program of Jewish music in a German church. Noticing that Maria was weeping, a Dutch colleague asked me if Maria was Jewish. She had strong emotional reactions to works of art and music.

Maria's father had died when she was eight years old, a traumatic experience that affected her deeply. Her mother, Mary Tunny Harris, taught in the New York City school system to support Maria and her brother, Tom. The family was a close-knit unit. Maria got much of her winning personality and energetic drive from her mother. Mary Harris died in 1991, at the age of ninety-three. She suffered from dementia in the last few years of her life (the majority of people over eighty-five have some degree of dementia). She was in a nursing home for about five years. I can picture Maria singing to her mother amid the cacophony in the nursing home. Her mother was seemingly at peace but not conscious of what was going on around her. But the sound of Maria's singing would light up her face.

Maria's brother, Tom, was a gentle and kind man. Maria thought the world of him, and they remained close throughout their lives. Tom had been head of the pressman's union at *New York Times* and he patiently dealt with the seemingly endless difficulties that his wife had. He had just retired at age sixty-seven to take up some serious golf when he was struck down with dementia. One Sunday morning on returning from church he could not put his car into the garage. His decline was precipitous from that moment. It involved violent behavior, something utterly out of character for him, but a phenomenon not uncommon among men with dementia.

Tom had to be moved four times because the hospital or nursing home could not handle his behavior. I remember one particularly harrowing experience when visiting him at Pilgrim State Hospital on Long Island. I had the impression that each place he went tried new drugs to control his behavior, but the drugs quickly made things worse. When I went over his autopsy with a psychologist, I said that although it listed three causes of death, I thought what killed him were the drugs. She said, "I think you're probably right."

At least the end was peaceful. I have a vivid memory of our visiting him in an ICU of the hospital where he died. A local priest known to both Maria and myself happened to be there at the same time. He said the Eucharist for the three of us at Tom's bedside. It was a religious moment that Maria always cherished. After Tom's death, Maria would say: "I don't want people saying he is better off dead. That may be true but just don't say that to me now." She mourned deeply this last member of her immediate family.

She was also concerned that Tom had died of dementia and that the disease seemed to be at least partially genetic. Maria had read that if a sibling dies of dementia, one's chances of having the disease increase by fifty percent. Maria was brilliant—except at math. I had to assure her that the statistic did not mean that she had a one-in-two chance of having the disease. I said that if five percent of people have dementia, then a fifty percent increase would mean that seven and a half percent of the population would get it. Her chances went from one in twenty to about one in fourteen. (I wasn't sure what the statistics meant, but at that time I was sure her anxiety was exaggerated.) The more important thing, I argued, was that she was a most unlikely candidate for the disease. It would not hit an active, healthy, intelligent, and creative person. I was dead wrong.

Maria and I had met in 1966 at Manhattan College. I said in her eulogy that within five minutes of our first meeting, we both knew that our lives would be entwined forever. That proved to be true despite some rocky moments in the early years (nearly all of that my fault). Our first book was written in 1967 and caused some stir. We wrote together when opportunities presented themselves. We also team taught when we could. Our first attempts at team teaching were fairly disastrous. I remember a course we taught at Fairfield University in 1975 that was awful. We each hit the students with everything we had. Eventually, we learned to adjust to the rhythm of the other; our styles became complementary rather than additive.

At first, I was the one with the most invitations to speak, and Maria came along as the junior partner. Rather quickly, she became the famous person, and she would bring me along as part of the package. We used to describe our approach as good cop/bad cop. She was adept at relaxing and engaging a group of people, so that my more formal approach had a chance of working. I learned a lot about teaching from her, and I still use some of her techniques in my classes. She was also the editor for everything I wrote. She was excellent at editing and was inevitably right when she gently criticized my harsh tone or vague abstractions.

We were professional colleagues as well as loving partners. She used to tell people that we would spend two hours talking at breakfast. And then in the evening we would have the same conversation and get paid for it. That wasn't exactly how it worked, but our last book, *Reshaping Religious Education*, actually did get written that way. In 1998, on the way back from teaching in Australia, I suggested we simply write down the table talk we had been having about our teaching.

In April of 2005, I was interviewed for an oral history of the 1960s catechetical movement. They wanted me to talk about Maria's part as well as my own. Maria's main influence came later; mine was largely confined to the '60s. I said in the interview that my voice in Catholic Church reform was effectively silenced by 1973—just as her voice began to be heard. I did feel that the things I cared about were not out of the picture. Maria and I collaborated on everything so that indirectly I still had a voice. She could say things in a way that did not alienate people. Even when she advocated fairly radical things her opponents found it difficult to dislike her. Except when bans against me occasionally spilled over to her, she was always and everywhere in demand. In the '70s she could playfully introduce herself as a priest of the diocese of Boston; no one missed the serious point she was making with a touch of humor.

Maria had a very different effect on men and women. She could charm most men right out of their socks. This included a fair number of bishops with whom she disagreed, but who never banned her appearance in their dioceses. In her eulogy, I told the story of one of the most conservative cardinals in the U.S. church who took a shine to her. I don't think he had a clue as to what she was talking about. He called her aside and told her she could call him "Father John." She received friendly notes afterward. I would often ask her what she and Father John were up to.

As for her effect on other women, I never sensed jealousy or envy. I think this was because she saw herself as speaking within—and for—a sea of sisterhood. She was at her best in giving encouragement to young women she met in the course of her travels. She had a talent for spotting bright young women who were on the shy side and just needed a little encouraging to let their light shine. She did not make a project of such people; it just seemed to happen. She would become friends quickly and deeply.

To this day, it puzzles me how she did it. Strong bonds of friendship take time to develop and require continual cultivation. I cannot figure out how she had enough time to sustain so many lasting friendships. When she was with anyone, she conveyed a sense that he or she was the most important person in her life, and for the present they were. At the funeral, several people said to me jokingly: "And I thought I was her best friend." I have a list of women in many U.S. states and several foreign countries who were her "best friend."

The fifteen years before her illness was an idyllic time for us. We were about as happy as human beings can be. Both of us were doing what we loved to do and what we believed was important work. We traveled to many parts of the world and met wonderful people. We lived in an apartment in Greenwich Village that was subsidized by NYU and we had a home in Montauk at the tip of Long Island. We had the best of city life and our small piece of paradise by the ocean. I picture Maria sitting in the hot tub in Montauk on a cool fall evening. She has a glass of wine in her hand and is saying, "How could a couple of people like us possibly be so lucky?"

Was she wrong about our being so lucky? I don't think so. For her part, she had a long and full life. Her death surprised people because she was so full of life. But the seven decades she had is a longer time than the vast majority of the human race gets. More important, she had a life rich in joy that spilled over to the numerous people she met. Her life exemplified the sacramental principle she so often spoke about, the spiritual embodied in the ordinary joys and sorrows of life. For my part, I was lucky to have the years we had together, and I feel nothing but gratitude for this grace in my life.

A single moment in Good Samaritan Hospital toward the end of Maria's life captures a central characteristic of hers. She was no longer able to do anything for herself and could not carry on a conversation. I would turn on music to which she did not react, but which I felt sure she liked. I would sit in silence next to the bed, not knowing what else to do. On this day I decided at noon to go downstairs and get some lunch. I did not know if she would understand my words, but I always spoke on the assumption that she could comprehend. I told her that I was leaving to go downstairs but I would be back very shortly. She looked up at me and said as clear as a bell, "Is there anything I can do for you?" I almost fell over because at that point she could hardly get a word out. As far as I can recall, that was the last complete statement she made. Friends who heard the story agreed that it was a fitting sentiment as a last expression. The essential kindness and goodness of her person shone through until the end, despite the ravages of a terrible disease.

CHAPTER ONE

Church: A People

*No image has so captured our Christian imaginations in recent years
as has the image of ourselves as a people. Although various models of
the church, such as herald, servant, institution, and congregation continue to influence us, the dominant self-understanding is increasingly
the church as a people.* —Fashion Me a People, p. 23

So begins Chapter One of Maria Harris's book. Those two sentences
set the context and the content of everything that follows. She lists
church models drawn from Avery Dulles's book, *Models of the Church*.
But her preference for "a people" is based upon the biblical phrase
"the people of God" (Deuteronomy 7:6; 1 Peter 2:10). Both the
Second Vatican Council and the World Council of Churches highlight-
ed "people of God" as the description of the Christian Church. The
phrase "a people" is not a simple statement of fact, akin to saying that
the church is many individuals or a big group. "A people" is meant to
suggest persons united by bonds of common origin and destiny.

As used by Vatican II and the World Council, the "people of God"
makes explicit the claim that the church is a people defined by its
relation to God. But while "a people" may seem to say too little, "the
people of God" is in danger of claiming too much. Although "the
people of God" is more liturgically and catechetically engaging than
other theological models, we should be aware that the phrase is likely
to strike an outsider as extraordinarily arrogant. Christians have a
right and a duty to use a rich language of intimate terms within the

church walls, but these days the walls are permeable. It is not only, for example, that many Jews read papal documents, but that Christians themselves live on both sides of the wall. Every Christian needs to be bilingual, on the one side enthusiastically singing Christian hymns but on the other side ready to live his or her religion in the secular language of today.

Maria's choice to begin simply with "a people" is not a denial that this people is of God, but she leaves the relation implicit. An educational approach begins from what can be seen and touched and heard. How the church is a people of God or more presumptuously *the* people of God has to be worked out in careful theological language. But the claim that the church is "a people" is a fairly modest claim, one that can be supported by historical evidence. From its beginning, the church attracted people from every social rank to form a new people that puzzled outsiders. It engaged the great philosophical minds of the world while it also cared for the most vulnerable individuals. Despite its failures to live up to its vocation of holiness, the church can still challenge in contrasting ways those who think themselves mighty and those who are oppressed by injustice and sickness.

The word "church," as I have used it up to now, contains several ambiguities. In Maria's first two chapters, she discusses several tensions that I will comment upon: local and global, clerical and lay, prophetic and priestly. Each of these tensions is in danger of creating a dichotomy in which the word "church" gets used for one side of this split. For example, "church" is often a reference to the clerical part of the church. Overhanging all of the tensions that Maria discusses is the main ambiguity in the use of church in this country: the split between Protestant and Roman Catholic.

The first issue, then, is whether it makes sense to speak of "the church." Should one instead speak of "churches"? I would say that whenever anyone in the United States says "church," he or she should consider whether the statement applies to both Protestant and Roman Catholic churches. I see nothing wrong in saying church when one is speaking of one's own church and addressing members of that church. But one should never speak in a way that explicitly excludes other Christians from sharing in the word "church" (something that both Protestants and Roman Catholics routinely did for centuries). And occasionally one should acknowledge either a wider meaning of church or a multiplicity of churches.

Maria does not name this tension within the church but her whole book manifests a keen awareness of it. One of the great accomplishments of *Fashion Me a People* is that it has been equally well received by both Catholic and Protestant readers. Very few authors have successfully bridged the Protestant-Catholic difference in educational language. Perhaps John Westerhoff, Thomas Groome, and a few other writers have succeeded, but Maria offers an extraordinary example of how to speak and write ecumenically. True to her deep Catholic roots, most of her references are to Roman Catholic sources. But teaching for eleven years in a Protestant seminary and speaking to numerous Protestant audiences made her very comfortable in referring to Protestant educational practices and literature. She not only knew but also appreciated Protestant education. Catholic audiences could quickly recognize her as their own. With Protestant audiences, she needed time to build trust, but by the time she wrote *Fashion Me a People*, her voice rang with a Christian truth that engaged Protestant as well as Catholic.

There has been wonderful progress in the cooperation of Catholic and Protestant educators for which one can be grateful. Big differences nonetheless remain. In the study of sacred Scripture, Catholic-Protestant differences are slight. In theology, there are some contrasts along with common themes. In education, a gulf remains between the world of catechetics and that of Christian education. I don't think that is all bad. There is no homogeneous Christianity that can be fed to youngsters and to old and new converts. The educational differences are a valid reflection of reality. Still, I think more attention could be paid to what can be learned from the differences. Catholic educators need time to talk among themselves about formation in the Catholic Church. Protestant educators likewise have to be concerned with their own denominational work. But if these conversations remain completely parallel, both Catholic and Protestant educators are missing out on helpful insights for their work and for Christian living.

Maria writes of three tensions within the church: local-global, clerical-lay, and prophetic-priestly. In each of these areas, there is a different approach taken by Protestants and Roman Catholics. All three were areas of conflict that led to the sixteenth-century Reformation. To this day, strong differences of emphasis are embodied in the functioning of churches and their educational practices. As a Catholic, I view the Protestant Reformation as a positive step in the development of a diversity of church forms. The division between Catholic and Protestant is often called a scandal; certainly when differences lead to violence, there is no longer a fruitful tension. The choice is between violence and education, which is why the trained educators in Catholic and Protestant Churches have a special responsibility to listen to each other.

Local and Global

We may champion the idea of small house churches and basic Christian communities alert to their own contexts and circumstances but only in the context of understanding that each local community will forge its identity in terms of its global relations within the entire church. —Fashion Me a People, p. 31

Maria rightly begins with the tension between local and global. More than the other tensions within the church, the local-global refers to a tension about the meaning of church itself. And it is where Catholics and Protestants need each other—so as not to collapse a tension built into the meaning of church from its origins. Some noticeable shifts of meaning have occurred in the last forty years, but Catholics and Protestants still usually mean different things when they say the word church. In the tension described as local and global, Protestant emphasis is on local, Catholics tend toward global. Neither side is unaware of the other side of the contrast, but they tend to fill it out with words other than "church."

Protestants refer to their local congregation as the church; beyond that there are regional boards, denominations, missionary societies, and numerous organizations that are involved in the global Christian effort. Catholics typically refer to their local congregation as the parish. When they refer to the church they may have in mind a building, a diocese, ecclesiastical officials, or Vatican bureaucracy. The Catholic usage has been changing, partly under the influence of Vatican II and partly from conversations with Protestants. Some Catholics do refer to their parish community as their church but that runs up against a settled way of speaking in which the large organizational structures can dwarf the parish assembly.

The Jesus movement that became the church started with a small assembly of Jesus' disciples and followers. The Acts of the Apostles describes the church's meeting in someone's home (2:46; 12:12). In the tension of local-global, the local has an obvious precedence. Global aspirations could only emerge when the church actually existed in one or several places. The Hebrew Bible referred to Israel in solemn assembly as the *qahal* of God. The Septuagint translated the term as *ekklesia*, taken from the voting assembly of the Greeks. The Christians immediately latched on to this term for their self-description, as indicated by Paul's addressing "the church of the Thessalonians in God the Father and the Lord Jesus Christ" (1 Thessalonians 1:1; also 1 Corinthians 1:2; 1 Corinthians 11:16; Romans 16:16). From the very beginning, the church was a people gathered under the sign of the "Christ followers."

The Local Church

The term "local church" has been coming into Catholic usage either as a substitute for or as a clarification of parish. If a global meaning of church dominates, the tendency is to think of the enormous organization as having regions, territories, or districts. The word "parish" fits into that way of thinking; it refers to geography, a space bounded by other space. When I first met young men from New York City, I was fascinated by the fact that their answer to "Where do you live?" was not New York City, Brooklyn, or 168th Street, but "St. Jerome's" or "St. Augustine's." The parish created the boundaries of a Catholic's life.

I do not wish to belittle the importance and the power of the parish. But it achieves its significance as it becomes more than an organizing district, as it becomes a *locus* or place. The parish becomes a local church as space becomes place. Walter Brueggemann notes that "place is space in which vows have been exchanged, promises have been made, and demands have been issued." A local church is one that puts the emphasis not on the building or the geographical territory, but on the people. As Vatican II's document on the church said, "the Church of Christ is truly present in all legitimate and local congregations of the faithful." The local church is the whole church in microcosm.

Parish can still make sense in many central cities. It may not be the defining element it was in the 1890s or the 1950s, but it may still offer an island of stability for the people of an urban neighborhood. If a parish is closed, sending people another twenty blocks to the next parish may seem a trivial change. But this other parish is not their place—their local church. I sympathize with officials who are trying to cope with financial problems and a lack of personnel. But a global church has to do something more imaginative than circle the wagons and try to keep the present system afloat.

In many U.S. suburbs, the parochial system is in disarray. Despite that—and sometimes because of that—some local churches are thriving. Many Catholics have decided for themselves that their local church is a place different from their parish (a recent poll found this to be the case with one out of five Catholics). The result can be ethnic, educational, or economic segregation. Such segregation was not uncommon with the traditional parish but individual choice was not the cause of it. There has to be concern for what may emerge as this process accelerates.

In my experience, the most vibrant local churches are found on university campuses. It is true that they can be islands of privilege and enamored of their own aesthetics. However, many university-based churches attract old as well as young, people with little schooling along with PhDs, a congregation with at least some shades of color. Perhaps the vibrancy of such places draws some of the lifeblood from surrounding parishes, but the answer to that problem is to increase the possibility of lively churches rather than lay blame on places that are real places.

The Global Church

The other side of the tension—the global church—is not in competition with the local church. To have a deep sense of the local is to feel a connection with people around the globe. However, I think there has been an unfortunate development with the terms "global" and "globalization." In the 1970s, globalization most often had environmental connotations. The plea to think globally was directed to taking care of the earth. These days, the economic meaning of globalization tends to overwhelm any other sense of the term. Concern for the global church could be misconstrued as support for Catholicism, Inc., ruled by the supreme CEO. The parish under the district manager would have to financially stand on its own or have its occupants declared redundant.

Catholic-Protestant cooperation is helpful in this context for two reasons. Up against what might be called the world's chief religion—capitalism—the Christian Church needs to present a united front. Except for occasional crises that have spurred some mutual support, the divisions within the church have obstructed unified resistance to the worst aspects of modernity. The other reason is the need for mutual reminders when thinking about a local-global tension. Because of its size and worldwide reach, the Roman Catholic Church is always in danger of forgetting that the local assembly is the church, an embodiment of the whole church. In the other direction, Methodists or Baptists are not in danger of mistaking church for a worldwide bureaucracy. But they need the challenge of asking how their churches are part of the church universal, the one true Catholic Church. Each Christian need not do everything; but each church has to act locally while thinking globally.

Clergy-Laity

In our time, sometimes imperceptibly and sometimes loudly and publicly, we are beginning to realize that the clergy-laity form of being the church is undergoing drastic revision.—Fashion Me a People, p. 33

Maria Harris is undoubtedly correct in suggesting that the clergy-laity tension is and should be undergoing drastic change. This division of the church was not part of its original constitution and does not serve well the current needs of the church. A clergy-laity structure was a stopgap measure that became a seemingly permanent feature of church organization. A clerical-lay split was a result of the church's fantastic success, starting with St. Paul's vigorous missionary activity that was more successful than he could have imagined. In the centuries that followed, the Christian movement brought in hundreds of thousands of converts.

The other side of the church's success in spreading the gospel was that education could not keep pace with the new and constantly expanding membership. A minority of well-educated members became the readers or clerics. The rest of the people, laity, received basic instruction from the readers. A church divided into readers and nonreaders was a necessity of another age, but it is inadequate in today's world.

There was and still is a need for various functions and offices in the church. Every organization of more than ten people has special roles and the need for someone to coordinate or direct activities. The New Testament already indicates a multiplicity of ways in which a person can participate in church life. Not a choice between clergy and laity but a range of a dozen or more ways of belonging to the church were available. The hardening into just two categories, clergy and laity, was an understandable but unfortunate adaptation to existing conditions.

One way to view the Protestant Reformation is as an attempt to transcend a clergy-laity division. The monastery started as a protest of brotherhood cutting across the clergy-laity split. Until the twelfth century, the monk was a third category of church membership. A saying in the early monastery was that the monks should avoid two groups of people: women and bishops. The monks were more successful at avoiding women. Monastic reform was constantly stymied by bishops ordaining the monks into the clerical class (hence the language of secular and religious clergy). Thus, by Luther's time the monk had migrated to the clergy side.

The sixteenth-century Reformation was not completely successful on this point. Eliminating the monastery did not automatically bring all Christians into a single community of brothers and sisters in Christ. While Christians occupied themselves with internecine warfare, the modern world emerged as a formidable sparring partner for a Christian worldview. The need was for a more sophisticated church education, but Catholic and Protestant churches could not get past a division between readers and nonreaders.

As I noted above, the distinction of roles is not the problem; the clergy-laity problem is that there is only one line instead of many. A two-class system is seldom desirable. In most such cases, including this one, an upper class is defined by what it has, the lower class by what it does not have. A certain irony surrounds the term "laity," derived from the Greek *laos*, meaning "the people." Laity could logically be the title of this chapter or be in the title of this book. What is the church? A laity (a people). The term began as positive and inclusive, but after the early centuries of the church lay and laity became negative in meaning. Any dictionary will confirm that laity and lay mean lacking in knowledge or skill.

The Christian Church succeeded in teaching the meaning of laity to the contemporary world. The distinction between professional and lay developed from the contrast between clerical and lay. In recent times, the church has tried to recover an older meaning of laity as the people. The Christian Church is probably the only institution today that tries to give a positive meaning to the term laity. The effort may be admirable but not one likely to succeed. The church is up against a nearly universal meaning of laity as a deficiency. More important, church writers do not seem inclined to go the full route to recover the original meaning of laity. That would require eliminating the category of clergy. If that were to occur, the church would still have readers (or clerics) but within the laity not outside it.

Cardinal Newman said it would be a strange church without the laity. Strange, yes, but perhaps desirable. As John Howard Yoder often noted, groups such as the Quakers are considered peculiar in not having a clergy but they might be better described as not having a laity. Newman's comment assumes a positive meaning of laity or the people. Yoder assumes the more common meaning of laity as lacking something. Church reformers therefore have a difficult choice because the options run in opposite directions: either accept the fact that a positive meaning of laity is unrecoverable and do away with the laity; or else, rehabilitate the meaning of laity so that the laity are the church. The former seems more likely to succeed, and it is a path that could create a more dynamic church while giving witness to a needed reform of modern professions.

The term that offers an alternative to clergy-laity is "ministry." Until Vatican II, most Catholics did not use the term. Occasionally there was reference to the priest's ministry but the idea of many ministries was foreign, that is, Protestant. Starting slowly with the Council, Catholics have taken to the term "ministries" and it is now helpful as a term common to Protestants and Catholics.

There is a misguided use of the term ministry as meaning everything that an individual does as a Christian. Like the word "education," ministry has to have an institutional form or else it will not bring about a rethinking of the church's overall form. If the term is to have a serious meaning, it has to involve a commitment by the local church and accountability by individuals involved. A five-minute commissioning of Sunday school teachers does not create a church ministry. In contrast, careful preparation of such teachers, perhaps with parish money to pay for workshops or graduate school tuition, would be a sign of mutual commitment.

The idea of church ministries does not work well if the term is simply superimposed on the clergy-laity division. Not surprisingly, that is just what happens unless there is strong resistance to the entrenched language of clergy-laity. Protestants have a longer experience with this usage of ministry but that has not really threatened the clergy-lay split.

The term "lay ministry" is a common phrase among Protestants and now sometimes found among Catholics. I would not disparage the many wonderful things done under the rubric of lay ministry. However, in the cause of long-term church reform, it is at best a transitional term. Given the positive and negative meanings of lay, the term lay ministry is either redundant or self-contradictory. If one assumes that the negative meaning dominates, ministry is an alternative not an addition to laity.

There should not be a church laity because each member should have a share in one or more ministries. Yoder writes: "Instead of ministry vaguely diffused through laity as a whole, why not specific ministries assigned to all members specifically. What is done away with is not specialized ministry but undifferentiated laity." In a local church of thousands of people, it may be unrealistic to have ministerial roles for everyone, but that fact is just an argument for smaller churches. A church member who wishes only to sit in the back pew on Sunday mornings should not be excluded from the church, but the word laity is unnecessary to describe a person who does not at present participate in one of the church's ministries.

Chapters Three through Seven of this book are about specific church ministries, within which there may be several ministerial roles. In some cases, there may be a single director or presider of a ministry. A person ordained to the priestly role would preside at the liturgy; a director of the church's educational programs might be in charge of a number of schoolteachers or catechists. One could use the term "ordination" for other ministerial roles than priest, though the Catholic Church does not seem inclined to go that route. Lacking a consistent language of ministry, the Second Vatican Council used a contrast between "ministerial priesthood" and "common priesthood of the faithful." While "priestly ministry" would make sense, "ministerial priesthood" makes no sense. That phrase freezes the term ministry in its pre-Vatican II meaning as belonging only to the ordained priest.

The term "pastor" has a long and special history in Catholic and Protestant traditions. Its biblical connotations need cultivating rather than the image of someone leading sheep. There is also a need to experiment with more than one pastor in a church. That suggestion can seem utterly unrealistic within the present system. In 2000, there were twenty-five hundred Catholic Churches with no ordained priest.

The seeming unrealism of having several pastoral leaders in the community is a sign of the need for changing the system rather than trying only to maintain it.

The church, like other institutions, needs order and patterns of authority for carrying out its work. A term appropriate to describe the church's pattern is "hierarchy," which means sacred order. However, the term was not first used for church organization. The original meaning of hierarchy was cosmic and mystical. As it was used by the author called Pseudo-Dionysius, hierarchy referred to the divine plan of creation: God at the center, surrounded by nine choirs of archangels and angels. On a circumference further out came the humans and then the other earthly creatures.

The image of the divine hierarchy or sacred order was circles inside of circles. This image makes a lot of sense today for ecology as well as theology, for organizational theory as well as metaphysics. This use of hierarchy can be found in Vatican II's reference to a "hierarchy of truths," the Christian message organized around its central truths including "Jesus Christ: the center of the history of salvation."

Alas, a different image of hierarchy came to dominate in its organizational applications. The Latin equivalent of hierarchy, *ordo sacer*, had first referred to the whole church, but by the fifth century, *ordo* was contrasted to *plebs*, the cleric was superior to the layman. As the twelfth-century church in the West shaped itself as a "perfect society," it spoke of a holy order (*sacramentum ordinis*). At first, this order referred both to the order of church organization and to the ritual for conferring the grace of deacon, priest, and bishop. Rather quickly, these three became orders or steps up a ladder of hierarchy. The image of hierarchy was a pyramid with the power to command coming from the top. The church taught this meaning of hierarchy to the modern world. A not-so-great legacy of the medieval church is that people can hardly imagine any other organizational image than a pyramid of power.

This chain of command from top to bottom can be efficient, at times indispensable. But hierarchy generally has a bad name. The people on the bottom or even halfway down feel oppressed by the weight above them. Even the man (usually) at the top feels isolated and powerless; in any large organization he cannot see what is going on at the bottom. He has to rely on a few trusted lieutenants who, because their jobs depend upon unquestioned loyalty to the boss, tend to shade the truth or withhold bad news.

I can understand why the modern secular world might have problems with the *hier* in hierarchy. Organizations do not wish to have a holy or priestly order. That is not the usual objection, however. The rebellion is against the exercise of authority in a pyramidic organization. People chafe at being subject to the arbitrary decisions of one other person and the feeling of impotence when things go wrong. The only alternative they can usually come up with is equality. But while equality is a legitimate demand for specific rights and privileges, it is hopelessly inadequate as the sole principle of organization and authority. What people hanker for is an expression of power that is mutual, an exercise of authority controlled by a basic unit of the organization that is communal. St. Paul (1 Corinthians 12:12–26) and Vatican II compared the church to the human body. The body has cells, tissues, and organs that have to work together without one part claiming to be superior. (Cancer cells are big shots in the body.)

The Catholic Church taught the modern world that hierarchy means a pattern of authority. But the Catholic Church seems to be the only organization that now regularly misuses the term in referring to itself. The standard usage of Catholics (which non-Catholics have picked up in speaking of the Catholic Church) is to refer to the bishops as the hierarchy. This way of speaking may seem like harmless shorthand in organizational talk. However, it is a disastrous misuse of language. Historically, logically, and practically, saying hierarchy when one means bishops makes no sense. The Christian Church is hierarchical, a holy order. Christian imagination is now being tested as to the imagining and structuring of this hierarchy. No issue is more important for the survival and health of the church. But the question cannot be asked, let alone answered, if one group in the hierarchy is called the hierarchy. No serious conversation about the Christian Church's holy order can take place with Protestants while Catholics continue to misuse the term. Catholics and Protestants cannot begin to explore how one might recover a hierarchy that is circles within a circle, or how the human body might serve as an image of hierarchical authority.

My objection to equating hierarchy and bishops is not an attack on episcopal authority. On the contrary, bishops are placed in an untenable position with their authority undermined if they have to carry the meaning of hierarchy. Authority belongs to the whole hierarchical body, each part of the body having its role to play. Bishops, too, are hierarchical members of the people who are the church. Vatican

II, by starting with "the people of God" and then moving on to "the hierarchical structure of the church" went in the right direction. But the significance of that move is undermined by the subsequent contrast between "the function of the hierarchy" and "the status of those faithful called the laity."

Priestly-Prophetic

Incorporating all the forms of ministry into our educational lives enables us to make that education a priestly one: a work of remembering, hallowing, and blessing. In addition, understanding all the forms of ministry also supports our prophetic vocation….Our speaking and doing are credible only if outreach and service are associated…with teaching, learning, and prayer. —Fashion Me a People, p. 45

In this third tension within the church, I have taken some liberty with Maria's formulating of the issue. In her second chapter, she describes the church's educational work as having the qualities of prophetic, priestly, and political. I have no argument with those three terms. They are a variation on what is said to be the threefold ministry of Jesus and the benchmark for all ministries in the church. What I suggest, however, is that the prophetic and the priestly are always in tension. And one way to refer to a fruitful tension is with the term "political." Priestly and prophetic clearly belong to religious history, especially Jewish and Christian histories. Political is a more questionable term, which in part of its meaning does not belong to church ministry. But the church cannot completely distance itself from the political dimension of life, even if it wished to do so.

The case for this tension was nicely put by Friedrich von Hugel in a letter to George Bernard Shaw: "In your play (*St. Joan*) I see the dramatic presentation of the conflict of Regal, Sacerdotal, and Prophetic powers in which Joan was crushed. To me it is not the victory of any one of them over the others that will bring peace and the reign of the saints in the kingdom of God, but their fruitful interaction in a costly but noble state of tension."

Von Hugel is taking issue with a body of nineteenth-century scholarship that posited a contradiction between prophetic and priestly. There was little ambiguity about which side of the divide had the better case: the prophetic was assumed to be forward looking, compatible with the march of European civilization into the future. The priestly, in contrast, was thought to be backward looking, sunk in myth and ritual. Once again, a Catholic-Protestant conversation is needed so that the priestly and prophetic are kept in tension rather than set in total opposition. The priestly has characterized the Roman Catholic Church, which has to learn to be more prophetic. Protestant churches have been on the prophetic side. Acknowledging the necessity of a priestly side may be difficult for some Protestant churches, but I mean here an attitude open to ritual and tradition, not an adoption of the trappings of the Roman Catholic priesthood.

Prophetic

The prophet was a distinctive feature of Israelite religion and the inspiration for all future prophets and prophecies. Being a prophet then and now can be a dangerous vocation. The prophet speaks hard truths that conflict with whatever is currently fashionable. Not surprisingly, anyone cast in the role is suspect. The ultimate proof of being a prophet is vindication by future events, but of course by then the prophet is dead.

The Hebrew prophets were said to be the mouthpiece of God, not an intermediary but someone in whom God's word resounds. The prophet's voice is therefore authoritative, which is not to be confused with authoritarian. A person who speaks with authority uses language compellingly. The hearer is free to respond as he or she chooses, but the prophetic words provoke engagement with the issue.

In modern usage, prophecy is thought to be about predicting the future. In contrast, the biblical prophet calls the people to renew the promises that they have made in the past. The prophetic word is oriented toward the future, but the word of the Lord unites past and future in the present. In the Bible, today (*ha-yom*) is decisive. "Today if you hear his voice….Choose this day whom you will serve." The present is not a disappearing point between past and future; the present is presence in which a community stands on the past and recognizes the possibilities of the future.

The Christian Church lays claim to the prophetic vocation. Like the ancient prophets, the vocation requires an authoritative voice that demands justice for all. Such words can and should be spoken from the pulpit, but what is said there will have little effect unless the church is on the side of justice in all of its works. The prophet's words may sometimes be directed at a priestly class, but the great sources of injustice in today's world are more likely to be business and political organizations. In any case, the prophetic is not a contradiction of the priestly.

Priestly

The priestly is concerned with the past. In the above passage, Maria characterizes it by the actions of remembering, hallowing, and blessing. When words fail us, at the beginning and end of life, in moments of great joy and deep sorrow, ritual holds together a community. The priestly gesture may be all that we can bear.

Religions, as Robert Bellah puts it, are "mortgaged to the past." They cannot cut loose from their own moorings, but without the tension springing from prophetic criticism, religions become frozen in time. The emphasis on priestliness should be on the character of a community, not the position of the individual priest. For remembering, hallowing, and blessing, someone in the community has to be appointed, ordained, or elected to the priestly role. Some people may be especially good at the role and grow into it throughout a lifetime (a vocation). But the community that is priestly generates a wide sharing of priestly possibilities.

The term closely associated with the priestly is "tradition." It is an idea that arose with the Pharisaic reform a few centuries before the Common Era. Strangely enough, tradition begins not with the priests, but with a criticism of the priestly class. Instead of taking on priestly authority based on sacred writings, the Pharisees laid claim to a second source, oral truths, and practices that had been handed down. This source, called tradition, was aural, oral, and tactile. Eventually, the Pharisees did transpose much of the priestly from the temple to the synagogue. And eventually, Jewish tradition was written down.

Tradition as the context for sacred writings can provide a more expansive basis for a religion. Without careful controls, however, tradition can be an excuse for justifying all sorts of practices that obstruct useful reform in a community. Martin Luther's attack was not on tradition but on the accretion of deadening traditions. In Jaroslav Pelikan's formulation, "tradition is the living religion of dead people, traditionalism is the dead religion of living people." Reform, including Luther's, usually consists in going deeper into the tradition. The reformer is profoundly conservative, as opposed to superficially conservative. The Anglican Archbishop William Temple wrote, "Few radical reformers can hope for great success who are unable to present themselves with perfect honesty as the only true conservatives." Unfortunately, by the nineteenth century, tradition had taken on a negative meaning, especially in educational literature, a theme to be explored later.

Political

I have suggested that the church's prophetic attention to the future and priestly hallowing of the past might be held together in the present political experience of Christians. Political refers here to the fact that the humans are speaking animals who have to work out their lives through interaction with people they may disagree with. Such political activity involves compromise and the protection of unpopular views. When churches try to avoid all in-house politics, the result is secrecy and the corruptive use of power. When the church tries to avoid interacting with the political structures of today's world, the result is a private enclave of the saved, rather than a church speaking vigorously to the high and mighty.

There is no denying that the church can get badly compromised by involvement in party politics. In the United States, churches are even legally bound not to engage in partisan politics. Like Jesus of Nazareth and numerous Christian mystics, the church has to take a radical political stance that challenges both the left and the right, conservative and liberal. I think that this is the message of Garry Wills's *What Jesus Meant*, though Wills is suspicious of all things political. It would be dangerous to distance Jesus' message from political life. Admittedly, politics can be dirty business; the litmus test for church involvement in politics is the maintaining of a tension between the priestly and prophetic.

Pope John Paul II was against priests holding political office even while he was one of the main political forces in the collapse of the Soviet empire. Joseph Stalin had contemptuously asked, "How many divisions does the pope have?" Mikhail Gorbachev knew well enough not to ask. In interviews of recent years, Gorbachev has said that the revolution in Eastern Europe would not have occurred except for Pope John Paul II. Similarly, Martin Luther King, Jr.'s rag-tag army of the disenfranchised proved to be a stronger political force than everything politicians could throw at him. King's priestly sense of ritual, along with his piercing prophetic message, was a peculiarly Christian form of political action.

Perhaps what the Catholic Church has to be asking is not whether priests should be in politics but how every Catholic Christian can share in some priestly and prophetic activities. Everyone does not have to do everything; there ought to be a variety of vocations within the church. And whole churches might put their emphasis upon either the priestly or the prophetic but be willing to cooperate with other churches that draw strength from a different strand of Christian tradition.

Occasionally there are extraordinary Christians who exemplify for the rest of us a startling combination of the priestly and prophetic. In the 1960s, Thomas Merton was an unlikely leader of the opposition to racism and war. Out of the quiet of the monastery came a voice of prophetic criticism fully relevant to the politics of the time. A Trappist monk in the maelstrom of politics was political engagement of a peculiar kind but one consistent with the greatest figures of the Christian past.

Church and Non-Church

A further implication of maintaining the tension between the local and the global...is our need to be in conversation and dialogue with religions besides our own. As the church becomes increasingly more conscious of the context in which it exists, we will be impelled more and more toward local Jewish-Christian, Muslim-Christian, and Buddhist-Christian dialogue and relations. —Fashion Me a People, p. 32

Maria Harris notes here that the global-local tension of the church is the embodying of the church's relation to all humanity. I return to the beginning of this chapter where I noted the seeming arrogance of the phrase "the people of God." While "a people" is not intolerant sounding, a Christian claim to be "the people of God" seems to disparage all who are not Christians. What can we say of the relation between "a people" who are the church and "the people" universally?

As Maria's passage indicates, the question demands at the least a conversation with other religions, and that is the main theme of this section. However, before getting to the relation between religious peoples, we need to take note of what may be a bigger tension among the peoples of today's world. Starting in the seventeenth century and especially throughout the last century, the phrase "a people" has been most closely aligned with nations and nation-states. Some nation-states are in crisis because they contain several national groupings, the nation being people who supposedly have a family connection.

An old European saying is that "a nation is a group of people who are united by a common error concerning their ancestry and by shared hostility to their neighbors." Nation-states could be just a convenient way to group billions of people. But religious trappings led to an ideology of nationalism. The birth and defense of the nation-state have regularly involved wars. "War made the state and the state made war," as Charles Tilly said. In wartime, countries talk endlessly of sacrifice, an explicitly religious term. And many citizens are ready to sacrifice their lives for their country. The nation-state gives people their sense of identity, inclusion, and mission. But in Raymond Arons's phrase, "No prince is entitled to make his country the Christ among nations." Unfortunately, that posture is the inevitable tendency of nationalism.

Arons's phrase suggests that the church, claiming to represent Christ, should lead the resistance to a militaristic nationalism. Sad to say the church has often been at the forefront of nationalistic wars instead of trying to de-idolize the nation. Despite past failures, there are few other organized powers in the world that might take on the task of opposing a destructive nationalism. The Roman Catholic Church with its world-wide reach and Islam's trans-national community (the *umma*), are probably in the best position to challenge the quasi-religion of nationalism. But every religious group has to ask itself: Are we a people in more than name only? Are we a people who are both patriotic (loving our country) and critical of our country's nationalistic disrespect of others? Are we a people trying to give witness to what peoplehood should be? These questions are not just for national leaders and church officials. The attitude and behavior of a people depend on all the people and the individual witness of each member.

From the beginning, the church has had to wrestle with the question of the outsider. Can one say, "we are God's gathering, elect, or chosen" without implying that everyone else is rejected by God? The answer lies in the peculiarity of religious logic in which the affirmation of the particular is the way to the universal. Jews, Christians, and Muslims have seen themselves chosen by God not because of their merits but as a witness to all peoples. The Bible and the Qur'an contain reminders that the real chosen people are the people, the human race. Jews, Christians, or Muslims are a stand-in for the people of

God. No one should get complacent or presumptuous about being God's people; ultimately, only God decides that.

The church ought not to play down its particularity, its distinctive doctrines and practices. The church is follower of the one who said, "I am the way and the truth and the life." In Christian language, the righteous of the world are on the path of Christ. Outside of a Christian context, that claim comes across as intolerant. Extramurally, Christians have to be prepared to speak a different language, one that does not contradict but complements the internal language. As Krister Stendahl puts the issue: "How do we sing our song to Jesus without telling dirty stories about everyone else?" The task is not so difficult if we avoid mistaking a love song for a doctrinal pronouncement. The passage from John 3:16, which is often heralded at football games, reads: "God so loved the world that he gave his only Son, so that everyone who believes in him may not perish but may have eternal life." The text does not say, "those who do not believe in him will perish." If the text is taken as a prayer of praise and thanks, it is compatible with a Christian praying that God so loved the world as to send the Qur'an.

An example of a well-meaning phrase that has been misunderstood and even ridiculed is Karl Rahner's "anonymous Christian." Rahner was simply trying to formulate what has always been integral to Christian belief and remains so. Rahner insisted that the phrase was aimed at Christian smugness; it was not designed for interreligious dialogue. It was an acknowledgment that non-Christian religions are salvific despite the belief, or rather included in the belief, that "Christ is the way." The phrase would be clearer though not so catchy as "anonymous follower of the way that Christians call Christ." It allows that other peoples have different names for the way; it says nothing about someone unknowingly being a church member.

When asked whether he would mind being called an "anonymous Buddhist," Rahner said he had no problem with that. "Anonymous Christian" is the highest compliment that Christian theology can offer, but what is offered as compliment can be received as insult. Given the misuse and abuse of the term "Christ" in Christian persecution of the Jews, I would not try complimenting a Jew as an anonymous Christian. In contrast, a Buddhist might understand the phrase as an offer of friendship.

For most of history, it has seemed sufficient to say with Peter in Acts 10:34–35, "I truly understand that God shows no partiality, but in every nation anyone who fears him and does what is right is acceptable to him." The community that claims to follow the teachings of Jesus should concentrate on living up to that ideal. If this way of life is experienced as valuable, there is an impulse to share it with others. As for those others who do not accept the Christian claim, that is God's concern and not for us to judge. The Bible and the Qur'an warn that we will be surprised at the final judgment to find out who the blessed are. Some of the Christians will not be church members, some of the true Muslims may turn out to be Christians. Rahner's "anonymous Christian" has some parallel to Calvin's and Augustine's doctrine of an "invisible church." Both formulas refuse to put a limit on God's grace.

A suspension of judgment about other peoples is still good policy but not a fully adequate one anymore. The intramural language makes its way not only into learned journals but also into the mass media. People of different religions interact with each other in the neighborhood or the workplace. Understanding religious logic and the paradoxes of religious speech aren't tasks only for a few intellectuals. Every Christian has to learn how to affirm his or her religion in a way that avoids needless offense and invites cooperation. The world cannot wait another century to work out a language of interreligious dialogue. Education within each religion and between religions is the great task of this century.

Educational Mission
and Curriculum

Education in the church is lifelong. This is too obvious to bear repetition, too obvious until we begin to see how major are the revisions this belief demands in our educational curriculum.
—Fashion Me a People, p. 38

With this passage, Maria Harris begins her second chapter entitled "Church: A People with an Educational Mission." I will comment here on Maria's second chapter and also her third chapter on educational curriculum. In these two chapters, she establishes the basis for the five chapters that follow on particular ministries. So that these educational ministries are recognized as important, we must first give serious thought to assumptions about education.

No area of life is so burdened with clichés that cover over with effusive praise society's ambiguous feelings concerning education. Society veers back and forth between glorifying education as the arrival of the messiah and disparaging the efforts of professional educators for doing child's play in the serious world of generals, presidents, and CEOs. When it comes to practical language for addressing problems and possibilities of education, the only thing that seems certain, especially to politicians, is that education is something good for six to sixteen year olds and it is given to them in schools. As Maria notes in her second chapter, it is difficult to alter this assumption, which is deeply embedded in our language, even when the enterprise does not seem to work anywhere near as well as we think it should. I think the genius of *Fashion Me a People* is centered on these two chapters where Maria proposes a framework that has a chance of breaking through the clichés.

Maria derived her five educational ministries from the text in Acts of the Apostles 2:42–47. She could have chosen other texts; for example, 1 Corinthians 12:27–31 or Romans 12:6–8 that more directly list the names of ministries. I think she chose her particular derivation because she already had in mind a correlation with secular educational forms. The correlation is not exact but, as she will show, it is quite close. I do not think, however, that she is subordinating the religious to the secular. So much of secular education is itself derived from Jewish and Christian ancestry. Unfortunately, contemporary writers on education miss out on getting help with their problems because they usually dismiss what they call "traditional education." The church's ministries do not provide ready-made answers for education but I believe that dialogue between secular education and church education would be mutually beneficial.

The educational framework that Maria uses fits comfortably with the catechetical work of the Catholic Church. The *General Directory for Catechesis* and the *National Catechetical Directory for Catechesis* were published after Maria's *Fashion Me a People*. Nonetheless, John Roberto notes that these documents have "a strong resonance with the five classical forms of Church life and their interrelationships as described by Maria Harris."

In this chapter I will draw two cautionary lessons from the history of education and religious education. I reflect then on Maria's concern with form and an educational curriculum of distinct but related forms. Finally, I use teaching as a test of these forms and whether this pattern can more effectively unleash the teaching possibilities of "a people."

Lifelong Education

It can be an experience both depressing and encouraging discovering that one's brilliant and original idea was already stated twenty, a hundred, or two thousand years ago. That doesn't mean the idea is wrong or that it won't work this time. It does mean that historical perspective is helpful in trying to avoid past detours on the way to a new world. Education has a long history containing brilliant new ideas, cycles of change, and slips of memory. At almost any speech on the big new thing in education, you can find someone at the back of the room muttering, "We tried that in 1987 or 1976 or 1955." Maybe it should be tried again, but with some chastened awareness of how difficult it is to change the way the human race operates.

Education in History

Our word "education" goes back to the Romans and a case can be made that education is coextensive with the history of the human race. The etymology of our English word "education" does not refer directly to children, as for example does the Greek *paidea*, a word derived from child. Throughout history, education has been closely associated with children for good reasons. The human infant, unlike other animals that are born with formed instincts, requires exorbitant amounts of time and constant care. As Jean-Jacques Rousseau said in the eighteenth century, everything not given by birth is given by education.

It is often misleadingly said that modern secular education and the church's education are focused too exclusively on children. Actually, education in the last two centuries tended to exclude children at their most formative and educable age. Most educational speech still assumes that education begins around age five or six (the language of "pre-school" strengthens rather than opposes that assumption). Both Rousseau and John Locke, the grandfathers of modern educational theory, have much to say about the education of infants, but that part of their theorizing disappeared in the nineteenth century. John Dewey, in the course of saying that the school must now take over what the family cannot do, describes the first stage of educational development as between four and eight years of age. Sigmund Freud and a host of successors have called attention to the importance of the young child's development, but our language of education has never recovered from the nineteenth century's turning over education to the elementary school.

The term "lifelong education" most often functions today as a synonym for adult education. That is not necessarily the intention of the user but without a rethinking of education from the beginning of life we just imagine adding more education to what happens to children of a certain age in school. Here is where a religious body could be helpful in insisting that the two most crucial moments of education are being born and dying; education begins no later than birth and ceases no earlier than death.

In the nineteenth century, an adult education movement began almost simultaneously with the spread of universal schooling, that is, with the legal pressure to see that everyone between six and sixteen years old attends school. Leaders of the adult education movement were in fact the conservatives, trying to keep alive the idea that education is lifelong. Authors at the beginning of the twentieth century predicted that by the end of that century education would have a very different look. Every town would have an educational complex serving the whole population around the clock. If these authors were to come back at the beginning of the twenty-first century they would be most struck by the fact that the language and system of education were so little changed. They would be surprised by a few things, such as the number of young people in college and the technology in the classroom. Otherwise, discussion of education would sound remarkably familiar.

The failure of the movement to refashion all education resulted in part from adult education in the twentieth century unwisely fashioning itself as the opposite of child education. Theorists of adult education declared that the child is dependent, the adult is independent; the child is to be taught, the adult is to be facilitated; the child learns subjects, adults are problem-oriented; and so on. The meaning of adult was modeled on the independent, individual, rational, middle-aged male. The theory and practice of this adult education made its way into the Christian Churches.

In the Catholic Church, both the *General* and *National Directory for Catechesis* say, "Adult catechesis should be the *organizing principle,* which gives coherence to the various catechetical programs offered by a particular church." The worrisome thing is that the passage goes on to say that this adult catechesis "is the axis around which revolves the catechesis of childhood and adolescence as well as that of old age." Note that "old age" is excluded from adult catechesis, a key test of the ideal of adulthood which is being assumed.

There is nothing wrong with taking note of special problems that may exist with the "education of the elderly." But a religious meaning of adulthood should include dependence, communality, and mortality that become more obvious as a person ages. The culture's exclusion of old age from adulthood is revelatory of its rationalistic, individualistic, and consumerist mentality. It is a sign of a despairing flight from death. Every time that I make a reservation online and am asked whether I am an adult or a senior, I wonder when it was that I ceased being an adult.

Religious Education

Part of educational reform at the beginning of the twentieth century was a religious education movement. In 1903, four hundred of the nation's leaders came together to found the Religious Education Association. Its grand purpose was "to inspire the educational forces of our country with the religious ideal; to inspire the religious forces of our country with the educational ideal." Most of the participants were Protestants who were concerned about the decline of the Sunday school. From the beginning of the common (public) school, the Sunday school was conceived to be its complement. The denominational teaching of the Sunday school was to supplement what Horace Mann called the "common religion of the public school."

The founders of the Religious Education Association recognized the need for major change. They proposed to carry out their educational ideal with a three-pronged approach: by forming a coalition of Jews, Protestants, and Catholics; by professionalizing education in church congregations; and by putting religion into the curriculum of the public school. Their intention was admirable but the project required far more resources than they could ever marshal. The organization quickly became identified as liberal Protestant. The economic depression of the 1930s and the arrival of a conservative theology from Europe put a damper on the movement from which it could not recover. By the 1950s, Protestant seminaries and local congregations had abandoned "religious education" as a first language and had gone back to "Christian education." When Roman Catholics appropriated the term religious education, they used it mainly for educational programs outside the Catholic school. Starting in the 1960s, catechetics became the first language of Catholics.

The ambitious project of education having a religious ideal and religion having an educational ideal was bracketed as naive idealism. Religious education never took solid root among most Protestant denominations; it was the work of theorists about the church rather than the living language of the church. For their part, most Catholics have shown little interest in the history of a movement that, despite its attempted outreach, appears to be Protestant. Catechetical language, which many Catholics at first found puzzling and too academic, was found to fit nicely with the new liturgy while being in continuity with the older generation's education through the catechism.

A first cautionary lesson to be drawn from the history of religious education is that educational language in the church has to be rooted in language that is familiar and particular to the group. Theorists cannot simply dissolve historic differences with comprehensive categories that will come across as abstract. That said, it is unclear to me that Christian education and catechetics must forever divide Protestant and Catholic educational worlds. The current usage of those terms is of recent vintage while both terms have a more inclusive meaning in the long historical past.

The language of catechetics goes back to the origins of Christianity. In Protestant history, Luther wrote the first catechism, and catechist and catechizing was standard Protestant language for centuries. If Protestants are at present unaccustomed to talking catechetics, that is still not an excuse for a Catholic use of catechetical language that excludes Protestants. As for Christian education, the term should obviously not exclude Catholics. The term Christian does exclude Catholics in many parts of the United States (while in some countries, Christian education is practically equivalent to Catholic education). Christian education as a term goes back at least as far as the Greek Fathers of the church. Protestant educators would do well to reflect on why Christian education literature includes almost no references to Catholics.

Maria Harris wisely sidestepped any direct confrontation with these differences. For naming educational ministries, she uses the one source that Catholics and Protestants could clearly agree upon, the New Testament. Some people might still find bias in the names chosen. For example, "liturgy" is more often used by Catholics than Protestants. The term carries connotations of elaborate rituals and vestments, things that have been criticized by Protestants from the beginning. Some conversation and mutual criticism could be helpful. It is noteworthy that the catechetical is not one of the ministries that Maria lists. No denial of catechisms and catechizing is implied, but other forms of teaching deserve to be explored.

The second cautionary lesson I draw from the history of modern secular education and the religious education movement is that adult and lifelong learning have been advocated for well beyond a century. Church educators picked up the cry of adult education from their secular counterparts and they were even more insistent. One can find books in every decade that announce this new idea of adult education. The church, it is repeatedly said, has just discovered the need for directing its attention to the adult community. Nearly every major writer on church education from 1910 onward has a variation on that announcement. Perhaps that is the best an individual author can do: point out hopeful signs of recent programs but with some historical perspective on the difficulty of changing educational patterns.

It must be made clear that we are not simply talking about extending education through more years. Many people react negatively to the image of forever sitting in a classroom. Describing education as lifelong is ineffective unless education is also life wide. The big change is not that education lasts longer but that it is a different kind of experience, based on the interplay of forms of ordinary life. This image requires careful consideration.

Educational Forms

Education, like all artistic endeavors, is a work of giving form. More specifically, it is a work especially concerned with the creation, re-creation, fashioning, and refashioning of form.
—Fashion Me a People, p. 40

One can easily miss the profound significance of talking about forms of education. Maria's statement above points out two important dimensions of these forms: education is the art of shaping these forms, and the educator is always re-fashioning forms that already exist in some shape or form. Note the paradox in the idea of fashion me a people. Who is being told to do that? How can the people fashion a people? Don't there have to be people before they can be fashioned?

A people is always being re-fashioned by the work of artists, saints, and ordinary laborers. The forms that constitute the stuff of education are what Ludwig Wittgenstein calls "forms of life," the ultimate organizers of human and nonhuman life. (It is significant that in earlier English one could educate a horse or educate a tree; life has forms beyond the humans). For example, the family is a basic form of human life; no form of life is more important educationally. Education has to start with the existence of the family, respect its built-in patterns, but ask whether some improvement in the form is possible and desirable. (Perhaps a shift toward mutuality of power between parents.) The form of the family can change only as it interacts with other main forms of life, but intrusions by social workers or church ministers have sometimes undermined the family.

For illustrating the meaning of form, Maria draws on what artists do when they take a given material and reshape it to bring out a beautiful design. The favorite metaphor of Greek philosophers for the meaning of form was the shape of a statue. When Maria taught, she used a wide range of artistic materials. She was especially adept in bringing music into her teaching. She also regularly used slides of great paintings and architecture.

In Chapter Two, she draws on her favorite exercise, working with clay. She would blindfold people and have them play with a big slab of clay. When she started using clay in the classroom I was skeptical that adults would go along. I never ceased to be surprised at the eagerness with which grown-ups would go searching for form in the clay. Any number of forms are potentially present in the clay but what emerges is the work of human hands, and as the blindfold suggested, the result is not necessarily what was aimed at. Education that is a play of forms cannot guarantee what the resulting product will look like.

The main educational forms are social in nature, the form that peoplehood takes and the forms that refashion a people. For clarifying the idea of educational forms, it may help to contrast this pattern with one that may seem similar. In 1960, Bernard Bailyn published an important monograph on education in seventeenth-century Massachusetts. Bailyn's question was how were people educated in the British American colonies. He found four "agents" of education: family, apprenticeship, school, and church. Contemporary theorists who do not want education limited to school often invoke Bailyn's historical research for support. Certainly, the picture he draws does undermine the naive assumption that schools are the only agent of education. Although the colonists started founding schools as soon as they landed (the ability to read the Bible was a paramount concern), the school had to be complemented by other institutions.

Among those institutions, the church was a major player. Even non-Christians had to attend Sunday service and listen to the sermon. It should be noted that Bailyn was not offering a "model of education." He was simply describing what the colonists brought from Europe, a pattern that immediately began to change in the new circumstances. Some Christians today might look back nostalgically to this time when the church occupied a prominent place in education. But when

the church was considered by society to be an agent dispensing education, the church was expected to act in accord with the model that
Maria criticizes, that is, officials indoctrinating children (or adults
treated like children) to know the doctrine and obey the laws.

Maria offers an alternative pattern, based not on institutions dispensing education, but rather on education as an interaction of artistic and
social forms. With this pattern of forms rather than agents, education is
the whole church educating the whole church to engage in ministry in
the midst of the world. The church is therefore an educator by being an
interplay of forms to reshape itself and the world about it.

In his writing during the 1890s, John Dewey, like many intellectuals of the time, believed that the school could replace the church. His
"pedagogical credo" shows the transfer of religious sentiments, including missionary zeal, to schools and their faculties. The essay finishes
with the announcement that "the teacher is the true prophet and the
usherer in of the kingdom of God." If it were possible to construe
teacher here as referring to Moses, Jesus, or Muhammad, the statement
could make sense. But teacher, as everything that precedes it in the
document makes clear, refers to the teacher in elementary and secondary public schools. The other three agencies that Bernard Bailyn had
described—family, apprenticeship, church—were declared by Dewey
to be moribund. The school was to be the chief agent of social reform.
The burden on the schoolteacher of the young was immense.

One result of assigning education to the school was that the school
became the only supposed form of education. Thus we have the contrast between formal education (school) and informal education
(anything else claiming to be education). People who try to argue
that not all education occurs in school actually find ready agreement:
they are said to be talking about informal education. Educational
reforms that begin by asserting that education consists not only of
schools but also of a, b, and c never get very far. Everything that is not
the school disappears into vague formlessness.

The way to start thinking about education in the church and elsewhere is that there are forms of education, but school is not usually
one of them. The modern school is a large institution that can house
several forms of education. Most good schools provide a range of
artistic, athletic, and academic experiences. Teachers in school teach
in several different ways depending upon whether they are instructing
in math, conducting a choir, monitoring the cafeteria, counseling a

student, or conferring with parents. The form of teaching changes with the form of education.

Church, like school, is not usually a form of education. It is true that just as a one-room schoolhouse comes close to collapsing the meaning of school into a form of learning, so also a church of a few hundred or a few dozen members could function as a single unit of education. Still, even in the smallest churches there are differentiations of role and several kinds of educational experience for church members.

The problem for most Roman Catholics in the suburbs of the United States lies in the opposite direction. Church connotes a large impersonal institution, not likely to be confused with a form of education. But the good news is that a large parish or local church, if imaginatively organized, has the resources to provide all five of the ministries that *Fashion Me a People* describes. School is not one of those five but that does not mean that the school is unimportant for the church's work. A school can be a source and location for several of these educational forms.

John Dewey is not much help in naming forms of education. However, he does supply a meaning of education that Maria uses to articulate her own. In what he called his "technical definition," Dewey writes that "education is the reconstruction of experience which adds to the meaning of experience and which increases ability to direct the course of subsequent experience." Maria uses all four parts of that definition while sharpening each of them with simpler words. First, she proposes "reshaping" as more organic and artistic than Dewey's favorite word, "reconstruction." Second, for Dewey's "experience," Maria uses the more specific "life forms." The third phrase "adds to the meaning" is replaced by "with end" in the sense of purpose; all education has purpose built into it. The fourth phrase that replaces "direct the course of subsequent experience" is "without end," in the sense of termination or end point. A simpler and clearer meaning results, namely, education is the reshaping of life's forms with end and without end.

The tension between the two meanings of "end of education" gives a continuing impetus to educational work. The Talmud reminds us that it is not up to us to finish the work but neither can we remove our hands from the effort. And the New Testament embodies this tension, for example, in saying that "Christ is the end of the law," in the sense of purpose but not termination. As Dewey could appreciate, there is a religious dynamic intrinsic to the educational tension "with end and without end."

Forms and Values

The forms that shape the universal values of community, work, knowledge, and wisdom [are] family, job, schooling, and leisure.
—Fashion Me a People, p. 42

The above statement gives a brief summary of the educational language Maria is drawing upon. She then translates this pattern into forms of ministry that constitute church education. I think it will be helpful to develop this pattern of secular education so as to enrich the ecclesial language of the five chapters that follow in *Fashion Me a People*.

In this section, I am not arguing what education should be. Instead, I am claiming that this is what education is. Throughout the centuries and remaining to this day, people have received a lifelong and life wide education from the interplay of educational forms. The precise nature of the forms varies according to culture and historical era. Nonetheless, my intention is to get at the "ordinary forms of life," which nearly everyone experiences. Of course, education can be improved; making things better is intrinsic to the idea of education. But improvement does not come from bringing in something entirely new. The two main ways to improve education are to make each form a more complete embodying of the value it expresses and to bring educational forms into closer and deeper relations with one another.

Maria names the four main forms of education as family, job, schooling, and leisure. No doubt a case can be made for other forms, but a broad conception of these main four can encompass much of art, science, technology, politics, and religion. Each of the main forms is complemented with numerous related forms. Staying with just four main forms conveys a simple pattern of lifelong and life wide education. I would re-state the four as familial relations, academic instruction, job performance, and leisure activities.

Each of the four is a partial embodying of the universal values of community, work, knowledge, and wisdom. Familial relations express community; academic instruction conveys literate knowledge; job is a form of work; leisure activity is for the sake of wisdom. Each of the four forms is a partial embodying of the value. Each form can be improved but it also needs complementing by other forms. For example, familial relations as a form of community need a network of communal organizations, including neighborhood, friends, sports teams, business groups, and church activities.

At each stage of life, one of the four forms comes to center stage. The values represented by the other three do not disappear; they merely shift to the wings. Thus, early in life familial relations are the center of a child's education; the sense of community holds a preeminent place. But a child needs to be surrounded by the values of work, knowledge, and wisdom. Later, when academic instruction for the value of knowledge is central, there is still a need for a sense of community, work, and wisdom. Then when a person's main learning is in and through a job embodying work, he or she still has to be surrounded by the values of community, knowledge, and wisdom. And late in life, when leisure activities are most prominent, community, work, and knowledge should not disappear.

There can be a kind of syncopation of the ages in which a particular form predominates. Family is central to infant education; it may take center stage again as parental education, and then again as grandparental education. Academic instruction may be specially suited to older children and youth; however, for some people it can re-emerge in middle age or old age. The movement to and from center stage is one of the ways that the forms interact with each other.

Each of the values that are embodied—community, knowledge, work, and wisdom—can be a stand-in for the purpose of education. One can say, for example, that all education is concerned with achieving genuine community or good work. Each of the four, however, is vulnerable to a reductionistic tendency. Contemporary culture tends to collapse the difference between job and work. Throughout history work has had a much more exalted meaning than the modern words "job," "employment," or "occupation." We have great works of art; religious people speak of the work of creation; and liturgy is the work of the church. Work is what gives life meaning, the contribution one makes to the good of society. One's job—salaried or unsalaried—is at best a piece of work.

Some people are fortunate enough to experience their job as real work; it gives meaning to life and provides a good to others. For other people, the job is just for "making a living" (a phrase that once meant a lot more). They may find their more important work when they go home from the job. Progress in education is signaled when jobs have real meaning and when dehumanizing labor is replaced by machines.

Where labor-intensive activity remains inevitable (for example, in caring for an infant), education should move in the direction of sharing that burden.

Leisure activity is another idea that has suffered a reduction in modern times. Some people may even think that "leisure activity" is a contradiction in terms. Isn't leisure the absence of activity? While in earlier times, leisure was considered to be the fullness of activity, we now think of leisure as time off the job, an empty time (vacation). Greek philosophy and medieval theology thought that leisure was an attitude that produced a calm centering of the self. One could say that a job becomes more educational as it incorporates leisure.

Everyone does need some time off the job daily, weekly, annually, and if one lives long enough, as a stage of life. But leisure should not be just empty time or time filled with mindless activity. An older person who has retired from a job still needs meaningful work, whether it is painting, volunteering at a nursing home, or sitting in the sunshine with a grandchild. Many older people, freed from the constraints of a daily job, are finally ready for some academic instruction. Seventy-year-old people do not automatically become founts of wisdom, but a society is educationally deficient if it does not provide roles for older people to share what they know with the young.

One is not likely to discover the difference between job and work at the age of retirement. Part of a young person's education is preparing for a job. However, a young person should also experience work that is not a job but is done as service to one's community. I was taken aback a few years ago in discovering that the only meaning many students have for "community service" is court-mandated punishment.

The idea of service work as part of one's education found a footing in many Catholic schools in the 1960s. Some public schools picked up the idea in the 1980s and it found wide support—at least among adults, though not always among young people. I find the extensive literature on the topic to be a confused mess. It is not clear that one can get voluntary service by making it a school requirement. In Jewish and Catholic schools, the service is usually tied to the (presumed) religious commitment of students. Many students in public schools are also generous in serving the community, but the public school is always wary of getting too close to religion.

When the curriculum of education is simply equated with what goes on in the classroom, service to the community is tacked on uneasily. Perhaps instead of "military service" for the children of the poor, the nation needs a "draft" that would include a wide choice among forms of service but would be a sign that education involves doing work that serves one's community. The school, public or private, could be an organizer of this service but a distinction from the academic curriculum would be desirable. The church on this point could be a teacher of how service is to be understood and accomplished.

All Are Teachers

Churches are returning to the practice of seeing all aspects of church life as educative and educating and thus part of curriculum.
—Fashion Me a People, p. 59

In Maria Harris's third chapter, she calls attention to curriculum as the lifelong and life wide journey from birth to death. She suggests that this is a return to an earlier understanding of education and curriculum buried in church history and Christian memory. The idea that our education begins at the beginning of life might seem obvious. We know that a child starts learning at birth, if not before. We have whole industries and teams of academics that are intent on following the infant's learning.

"Learning" is nearly a sacred word in contemporary speech; no one proposes to vote against it. Not so the words "education" and "curriculum," which are usually consigned to buildings occupied by six to sixteen year olds. And in the United States of today, the words "teach" and "teaching" are downright suspicious, often negative in meaning. As I noted earlier, the adult education movement relegated the word "teach" to adults telling children what to think. Teaching in this context is imagined to be at best a supplement to learning and at worst an interruption of learning.

This peculiar way of speaking is in part traceable to a shift at the beginning of the twentieth century that gave over educational language to the emerging field of psychology. Like many others of the time, John Dewey was enthusiastic about the fact that psychology would finally make education into a science. Dewey's keynote address at the first Religious Education Association meeting was on the importance of the new psychology for religious education. Dewey's version of psychology, heavily influenced by William James, was a branch of philosophy. Dewey was stridently opposed to Freud's depth psychology on one side and to Edward Thorndike's quantified psychology on the other. While Dewey had considerable success in urging teachers to be psychologists, his own kind of psychology lost out in the history of education; Freud and Thorndike were winners. By the 1930s, Dewey recognized the importance of economics, politics, religion, and art in education but his view of education was still encapsulated in psychological concepts.

Psychology has made wonderful contributions to our understanding of learning. It has had almost no interest in teaching and teachers. The most famous theorist of the child's learning capacities, Jean Piaget, has nothing good to say about teachers. Their main job is to get out of the way of the child's learning. Piaget excoriates Emil Durkheim for implying that "the schoolmaster is the priest who acts as an intermediary between society and the child." For Piaget, the ideal is a child who becomes an autonomous individual. As soon as the child is ready, he or she should get rid of all teachers and teaching. Immanuel Kant, the intellectual ancestor of Piaget, wrote in his famous essay on enlightenment that every individual should "dare to be wise." Kant urges us to throw off our tutelage and think for ourselves.

In an effort to give support to teaching, academics in "teacher training" colleges devised experiments to discover what constitutes effective teaching. They tried to find a causal connection between behaviors of a teacher and learning by the student. The results were shocking. They could not find any cause and effect relation between teaching and learning. As a result, it has been unchallengeable dogma for the past half century that teaching and learning are separate activities; the presence of one implies nothing about the presence of the other. Teaching, which long had a tainted reputation in this country, was reduced even further.

The researchers should not have been surprised that they could not find a causal link between behaviors of a person at the front of a classroom and what happens in the minds of students in the room. I would think that any experienced classroom instructor is only too well aware of this disheartening fact. The poor instructor keeps pressing in on the students to shorten the gap between intention and result, usually only increasing the frustration of both instructor and students. In contrast, the good instructor keeps trying to discover what is teaching the students and how one might influence that; the result is humility on the part of the teacher and breathing space for the student.

The researchers' failure to find a causal connection led them to proclaim that teaching is one thing, learning another. A different explanation of their findings is that they started looking in the wrong place and assumed a much-too-narrow view of teaching and teachers. Classroom instruction is one very peculiar form of teaching, which can be successful only when the circumstances are just right. The more common kind of teaching is where teacher and learner succeed together or fail together. In a *Peanuts* cartoon, Lucy says to Charlie Brown, "I taught Snoopy to whistle." When Charlie says he has never heard Snoopy whistle, Lucy says, "I said I taught him; I didn't say he learned." Anyone can see that Lucy has a very restricted meaning of teaching. No one comes into the living room and announces: I taught Johnny to ride the bicycle—but he did not learn. Walking, talking, eating, singing, dancing, swimming, and innumerable activities are learned through an interplay of human bodies; the teacher and learner succeed together or they fail together.

Any attempt by the church to put forth a curriculum of ministries has to be aware of the narrow secular meanings of education, curriculum, and teaching. At times in the past century, church education has been nearly absorbed into psychology or at least it has assumed that education is mainly about the psychology of learning. The study of psychology can be a very useful tool. But while the relation of teaching and learning can be looked at psychologically, it is also a social, political, and religious relation. As Maria insists, the church cannot teach through its various ministries unless it recovers a richer meaning of teaching. That rich meaning of teaching is present in religious history.

Throughout history, especially as emphasized by religious groups, teaching is recognized as one of the most fundamental activities of all human (and some nonhuman) beings. Teaching-learning is a single activity, viewed from opposite ends. The test of teaching is learning; the test of learning is teaching. People are constantly learning because they are being taught, a fact that forces us to recognize all the teachers in our environment. Even in a classroom, the main teacher might not be the person at the front of the room. The architecture of the room, the time of day, and the other students in the class can help or hinder the efforts of the professional instructor. David Elkind makes the comment that the child classified as a slow learner is quick to learn that he is slow. The child learns that not because the instructor says so but because procedures in the classroom or the reward system of the institution convey his place. He is quick to learn he is slow because the school teaches him he is slow.

The root meaning of "teach," going back a thousand years in English, is to show someone how to do something. (English does have a problem in using such different words for teach and learn; in many languages the two words have the same root.) Most comprehensively, to teach is to show someone how to live, which includes how to die. Religions often begin by teaching people how to die because without the acceptance of mortality, a person can never fully live. We begin to die the moment we are born, a fact that is directly related to the narrowing of the meaning of teach to the giving of explanations.

It is no accident that the flights from teaching, death, and religion happened almost simultaneously. Teaching someone how to live and die is an acknowledgment that the universe is not under our control. It is an acceptance that every human teacher can only represent something bigger and older as the source of wisdom about living and dying. The idea of creation, as Thomas Aquinas says, implies that God is the supreme teacher and that everyone—and everything—can share in the power to teach.

Aquinas even says that the things considered least in human evaluation may be the most important teachers. Erasmus said his most important teacher was his kidney stone. The contemporary world tries to protect itself from reminders of creatureliness and mortality by restricting teaching to the exposition of math, science, and literature for children who are rational enough to understand but not yet old enough to think for themselves.

Teacher and Teaching

The greatest accolade that most religions have for their founder is "teacher," even though Moses, Gautama, and Confucius have very different styles of teaching. The religious tradition itself is said to consist of teachings. While this language is found in Christian history, there is a quirk in its early history that still affects the church. The New Testament is as clear as any religious document on the centrality of the founder's teaching. More than forty times Jesus is called "teacher" (though it is often translated as "master"). The verb "to teach" is also attributed to Jesus at least fifty times. As the *National Directory for Catechesis* rightly notes, "Teaching was central to the ministry of Jesus."

In Matthew 23:10, Jesus says to his disciples: "Do not be called teacher"; he says it twice using the Greek *didaskalos* and the Aramaic *rabbi*. Contemporary scholars understand the text as addressed to Jesus' inner circle of disciples that they should not adopt the outward trappings of other religious leaders. The text reflects the growing conflict between the rabbinic-led synagogue and the followers of Jesus. A political conflict over the title of rabbi had unfortunate and lasting effects on the Christian appreciation of teachers and teaching.

Jaroslav Pelikan, in his book *Jesus through the Centuries*, places "rabbi" first: The most universal and least controversial title of Jesus in the New Testament was "teacher." But, as Pelikan goes on to say, history took a different turn. "To the Christian disciples of the first century, the conception of Jesus as a rabbi was self-evident, to the Christians of the second century, it was embarrassing, to the Christian disciples of the third century and beyond it was obscure." In Augustine's treatise on teaching he cites the text from Matthew 23 to support his contention that no human being really teaches; only God is a teacher.

Every great church reform involves returning to the sources and recovering a meaning of teaching and teacher in which all Christians can share. Teaching is not something that can be relegated either to Sunday school teachers or to Catholic bishops. As Maria says, it is the whole church that teaches; it is the whole church that learns. Anyone who lays claim to teaching has to locate him or herself in the grand march of centuries and the worldwide play of educational forms.

It is often said in Catholic catechetical literature "the catechist is not a mere teacher." The intended point is understandable, but the formulation is disastrous in accepting the narrow connotations of teaching. Better to say that the catechist is nothing less than a teacher, sharing with parents, schoolteachers, artists, bishops, and others in the exalted teaching mission of Jesus, the Christ.

Discussions of teaching in the Roman Catholic Church are hindered by an obscurantist use of the Latin word *magisterium*. Its current usage goes back only to 1830. Since magisterium simply means teaching, the word was used throughout the Latin Middle Ages. There was a "magisterium of the professor's chair" and "a magisterium of the pastoral chair." The current use has the effect of trying to eliminate most forms of teaching in the church. How every Christian participates in "the church teaching" (as well as "the church taught") cannot be explored when a peculiarly abstract meaning of magisterium stands in the way.

The modern assumption that to teach is to explain makes teaching a talkative affair. But the talk is peculiarly one dimensional, its primary model being a big person telling a little person what to think or what to do. The rich resources of language go unexplored if one starts reflection on teaching by looking to the classroom. The great variety of ways of speaking that the church has used throughout the centuries is obscured by assuming that to teach is to tell. One cannot appreciate all of the teaching languages (storytelling, preaching, praising, thanking, confessing, forgiving, comforting, debating, criticizing) unless one goes to the root of all teaching: silence.

Most teaching in the world is nonverbal. The power of example trumps any speech to the contrary. The place to begin reflection on teaching is with a mother—human or nonhuman—showing the newborn how to survive in this world. Teaching is ostentatious, says Wittgenstein, one bodily creature demonstrating to another how to move the body. It is a wordless process at first, though a cooing sound may remove some of the anxiety that the vulnerable young understandably feel; this is not an immediately friendly world for finding warmth and food. The young are eager to learn and, lacking words to communicate their desires, attend to their surroundings in silent, rapt attention. Nonhuman animals never speak in a way recognized by us, and so they study humans carefully. They pay much better attention to us than we do to them.

No better example of teaching-learning exists than the human community demonstrating how to speak and the child responding by learning a language. Amid the cacophony of the child's surroundings, he or she responds to a human voice and matches speech with bodily movements—not just words for things but a structure of language responding to a human situation. Speech is one of God's greatest gifts to humans. It makes all kinds of great accomplishments possible. Literary arts and the whole range of science depend on language. More basically, language is the means by which humans share life and discover who they are. We find out what we think by carrying on conversations interiorly and with other people.

The one terrible danger with speech is that we can forget that it is born in silence and must be constantly refreshed in silence. No amount of talk can substitute for the well-placed gesture of the human body. Barbara Grizzuti Harrison recounts a moment in her early life that eventually led her to become a Roman Catholic. As a Jehovah's Witness, she would remain seated in school during the saluting of the flag. Other students heaped scorn on her, except for one boy, Arnold, who would sit next to her silently and hold her hand. Harrison said that his action proved to her that he was not wicked as her religion claimed.

We are surrounded by silent teachers, and a big part of education is learning to discriminate the good teachers from the bad. We don't have total control over the process of teaching-learning. A certain amount of bad teaching inevitably seeps into the soul. But humans are resilient and can overcome the bad with the good. As Fyodor Dostoevsky said, one good example from childhood may be enough to save us. Some of the good teaching affects our soul without our fully grasping that fact. We learn to live because we are taught by our own life experiences and by the vicarious experiences of art and narrative.

The great novel *Middlemarch* describes its heroine this way: "The effect of her being on those around her was incalculably diffusive; for the growing good of the world is partly dependent on unhistoric acts; and that things are not so bad with you and me as they might have been is half owing to the number of those who live faithfully a hidden life and rest in unvisited tombs." In this passage, author George Eliot has drawn a poignant portrait of how we are all dependent on acts of faithfulness and love in the lives of ordinary people. In choosing the word "diffusive," Eliot was undoubtedly aware of that word's history in medieval theology and mysticism. The doctrine central to moral thinking for

Maria Harris developed her own stages of women's development in *Dance of the Spirit*, *Jubilee Time*, and other writings. Her metaphor of development is the dance; stages of development are steps that are forward or back, in and around. Like development as a whole, each stage begins and ends in silence. In the interplay of stages, the silence that is the end of one stage can be the beginning of another stage. The process continues until the last stage is truly final and we find ourselves in the place where, as C.S. Lewis says, "All that is not music will be silence." Maria always pointed out that silence could be negative or positive. For the young girl who has never acquired a voice or has lost trust in her own voice, silence is oppressive. But there is also a fullness of silence, a silence of prayerful contemplation, which is human development at its best.

many centuries was "the good is that which is diffusive of itself." Goodness overflows, bubbles over, cannot be stopped from sharing what it has. The mark of the spiritual, said Augustine, is that it can be possessed only by being given away. To the question of why God created the universe, the rabbis answered: because he is good and goodness overflows itself.

Every act of teaching—first in silence and then with the help of words—imitates the divine creation. Every living being and everything shares in the diffusion of goodness by the activity of teaching. The church's teaching ministries are a reminder to its members of all that has been received and must be shared to be possessed. The church's mission is also to stand witness in the secular world to the profound truth that good example is the most powerful teacher.

CHAPTER THREE

✿
Forms of Community

I am proposing community and communion as the initial educational ministry….Only out of life together as a people do patterns of worship or programs for teaching or outreach make sense. The fashioning of a people does not occur unless a people exists to be fashioned.
—Fashion Me a People, pp. 75–76

Community as the first educational ministry may seem too obvious for saying. Isn't community simply another name for "a people"? The four ministries in the chapters that follow this one clearly flow from community. But that does not explain why community is a ministry instead of a precondition for ministries. Why does the *General Directory for Catechesis* say that church community is the content as well as the agent of catechesis? The answer lies in Maria's sentence above: the paradox that the community is both fashioner and fashioned. A people has to exist before its activities can take shape, but those activities in turn develop further the peoplehood or community.

For most of the population, community has a warm and positive meaning. No one gives speeches denouncing community. Politicians and advertisers love words that stir up some good feeling without calling forth any critical thinking. Community is often just rhetorical jargon. Instead of a framework of community, our science and politics revolve around the linked ideas of the individual and society. Communal forms such as the family and the household come into discussion only for gathering statistics and only as the grouping of individuals. The individual is the rock on which everything else is built; and society is the name for the everything else.

The term "society" goes back at least fifteen hundred years but for most of its history it referred to small groups with a specific purpose, as in a choral society or a burial society. The Christian Church had a big hand in the generalizing of society and turning society into the term it has become in modern times. Rousseau was one of the first students of this modern society. His view of society has been described as "the church without Christ." That captures the all-encompassing demands of modern society. We now routinely assume that politics, economics, or religion are within a big tent called "society." Society may bestow the word "community" on itself or any social group within itself, evacuating the specific implications that "community" might convey. In the context of educational ministries, the idea of community is a challenge to the dominance of society.

The claim that the church as community is an educational ministry involves a more precise meaning of community than the usual references. In Chapter Two, I described community as an ultimate educational value. Whatever sociologists call a community can only be an imperfect realization of the human community. That limitation applies to the church and churches. Education concerns the improving of forms of education so that they more fully embody community, as well as work, knowledge, or wisdom. That is why the church has to continue to be fashioned anew. Forms of education are living forms that are in a constant process of change.

What Is a Community?

Deep within the human heart is a longing for a holy time when all will be one, a dream of a new heaven and a new earth when death shall be no more, neither shall there be mourning, nor crying nor pain anymore. —Fashion Me a People, p. 76

In this passage, Maria Harris gets to the essence of community, an idea almost totally absent in all of today's talk about it. Pushed to its most profound meaning, community is unavoidably a religious idea. It exists as a longing and a dream, only imperfectly realized in actuality. Community refers to a particular form of human organization, one in which the group and the individual are affirmed together. Persons exist in relation to community, while community is a union composed of persons. Community unites and differentiates at the same time. Humans constantly glimpse the possibility of such union but they never fully experience it. The desire for community lies deep within the human heart but each group claiming to be a community falls short of a perfect realization of that claim.

The Christian Church lives in the tension between what is and what is to come. It must try to be perfect while acknowledging that human beings never are. This principle is important for the enforcement of laws in any group, including the church. Not only does there have to be some compassion for weaker members, the morally upstanding individual should not act as if he or she were living in a perfect community. Harm can be done to oneself and to others if one is not realistic about the communal limitations of one's group and the need for intelligent compromises. Paul had to urge such compromise to the church community of Corinth concerning eating idol-sacrificed meat (1 Corinthians 8:9).

The hallmark of community is mutuality, an interdependence in which the good of one is the good of all. In a perfect community, all things would be held in common, no one would be short-changed, and each person could exercise his or her creative powers. The obstacles to the realization of such mutuality are twofold. First, each person experiences a self-dividedness that interferes with a wholehearted self-giving. Second, the spatial and temporal conditions of human life set severe limits on the possibility of mutual exchange.

The first of these obstructions, self-dividedness, has historically been attributed by Christians to original sin. Jews and Muslims reject that idea and one must admit that a doctrine called original sin may convey misleading connotations. What no religion denies is that the human heart is divided, not that we are half good and half bad, but that there is an inner struggle to reach a unified self. We cannot be transparent to others because we are not transparent to ourselves. Economists who make predictions based on the assumption that people rationally choose their own good do not have a very good record. The term "person" has a double meaning. It means one who speaks, who finds fulfillment in face-to-face encounters with other speakers. But person also means mask; the face is always partially hidden. Language reveals some aspects of oneself and the surrounding world, but not without hiding other aspects.

Where mutuality is most clearly promised is in romantic love. Two people can feel as if they are one. Each may wish to be totally open, honest, and truthful about their lives. Sometimes the first feelings of mutual self-giving turn out to be illusory. Even a couple that stays together for decades may still meet surprises in what one person does and does not know about the other. Marcus Buckingham describes a study of happy or successful marriages, the results of which he calls counter-intuitive. The best marriages are not based on both parties being frank and accurately knowing their spouses. Good marriages, it turns out, depend on each party having an idealized picture of the other. Each sees the other party as a better person than he or she sees him or herself. One could say that love is blind but it is a peculiar form of blindness that sees the best in the beloved. Who is to say that the idealized picture is not a true possibility? Half of marriages these days end in divorce, but that does not halt the quest for true love. Some people do seem to find the love of their life, thereby giving witness to the fact that love is possible.

Love between two people does not constitute a community. Actually, in the search for community, the bond between two people often appears as a problem. The unity of a small group can be in conflict with love between two people. Here we meet the second obstacle to the realization of community, that conditions of space, time, and numbers set severe limits to the possibility of mutual exchange. If mutuality of persons is to be experienced, there has be actual presence of a group and the sharing of a particular place.

Does modern society offer any real examples of a community of persons? In contemporary speech, community most commonly signifies either a radical withdrawal of a group of people who think they can set up an alternate universe, or else the term is used for almost any sociological grouping, whether village, neighborhood, city, nation, or international organization.

Communal Experiments

Concerning the first of these meanings of community, the United States has had a constant stream of communal experiments, often called communes. Some eras have been especially fruitful, such as the mid-nineteenth century and the 1960s. The typical pattern of the commune has been a youthful flight from the urban industrial center for a quiet place in the countryside, the abandonment of private property, and a frowning upon sex. The rural commune has been the subject of much study. Less obvious and less studied is the urban commune with a greater range of ages, a more pragmatic view of property, and lots of sex rather than no sex.

Most of these communal experiments have a short lifespan. The ones that do last for more than a few years almost always are sustained by religious conviction. Without a belief in religious purpose, attempts to challenge the ordinary assumptions about sex, property, and authority inevitably falter when bad times come, as they do in everyone's life and in every organization's lifespan. When sexual activity is proscribed within the group, the choice entails the exclusion of children. The community cannot constantly regenerate itself with new members and is dependent on bringing in new adult members. Most religious groups that have excluded sex either end quickly or eventually find themselves with an aged population. (The average age of people in Catholic religious orders today is sixty-three.)

While a way of life that excludes sex may be a good interim choice for many people and a healthy choice for a minority, it has great limitations as a form of community. A demonstration model for humanity ought to embody a wide variety of color and class and include three generations and two genders. The world today still needs some thoughtful and well-designed experiments in community living. The task should not be left exclusively in the hands of rebellious twenty year olds.

The number of people that can form a manageable communal cell is severely limited by simple mathematics. It takes time to establish mutual relations and human beings have a limited amount of time. For the demonstration community to work, the number of people should be larger than the usual family size but small enough to allow mutual relations among all the members. That number usually cannot exceed a dozen. It is no coincidence that Jesus had twelve rather than forty intimate disciples. He did have a wider circle of seventy-two and indefinitely wider circles beyond that. But the core group was a chosen few.

The Village

Besides the commune, the other most frequent use of the term "community" is a warm-sounding word for almost any group of humans. Small towns like to call themselves a community, suggesting neighbors who are friendly and helpful to one another. Sections of a city are called communities to indicate a homey feeling like one finds in a small village. Minority groups that are called communities (racial, sexual, ethnic, political, artistic) indicate that they are in an heroic struggle against an oppressive majority. The phrase "international community" could be a cruel joke, except that it may express a hope for world unity in the face of much evidence to the contrary. In each case, one hears a hint of that longing for the time when all will be one, a dream of a new heaven and a new earth when death shall be no more. Despite all efforts to repress the religious dimension of community, it never disappears.

Many modern theories of ethics wish to turn our attention to all of humanity—the human community. While such concern is desirable, it has to be grounded in ordinary, practical concern for these two, five, or ten people. Lawrence Kohlberg's influential scheme of moral development placed concern for family members at a low level. At the top of his system was the man who could think impartially about all human beings. That Kohlberg could not find many people who reached the top of his scale was perhaps encouraging. A person who can abstract from all differences and treat every person the same may be lacking in emotional depth and moral sensitivity.

John Dewey, in *Democracy and Education*, proposed a twofold standard for community: the members should have many interests in common, and the community should have cooperative interaction with other groups. In his first criterion, he compares a band of criminals who have only the one interest of robbing a bank to the family's many intellectual, material, and aesthetic interests, which hold together the family members. Dewey also cites the family for his second criterion, that the family is related to business groups, schools, and many other institutions.

These two criteria of community are a help. But Dewey's standard of community, like his meaning of the religious, seems to be lacking in depth. Both criteria are concerned with manyness, which is but one aspect of human life. Dewey's thinking may be all too representative of contemporary thinking about community. The people in a small town where everyone knows everyone else's business may have many contacts, but not many deep ones. A celebrity who has a party for his closest three hundred friends may not yet have discovered friendship. People who have experienced community at a weekend workshop may have discovered the beginning of community. The test is in the weekends, months, and years that follow. Our fragile social institutions don't always have to be permanent but they do have to withstand the ups and downs of ordinary life, including sickness and health, success and disappointment. The standard marriage vows give fair warning to bride and groom.

Family as a Communal Form

I pointed out earlier that among forms of community, the family has always had a preeminent place. Our first and in many ways our most influential education comes through familial relations. The family can be the source of some bad teaching, some dreadful lessons that scar people for life. The family can also convey the deepest moral and religious sentiments that sustain people in dark times. The *National Directory for Catechesis* recognizes that "the Christian family is ordinarily the first experience of the Christian community and the primary environment for growth in faith."

The Second Vatican Council several times referred to the domestic church. A house church or a church in a family setting harkens back to the early history of the church. It is an idea much richer in Protestant than Catholic history. Each branch of the Reformation insisted that the family is the basic unit of the church. The Puritan founders of the British American colonies were insistent on each family being a domestic church headed by the father of the family. The great hopes of the first colonists were not to be realized. The perfect little domestic churches could not be sustained. As one historian said, the Puritans were brought down to earth by biology: children kept getting born and the process of conversion was always beginning anew.

The family has had an exalted position in the rhetoric of the British American colonies and the United States. However, children have not fared well throughout that history, including the present when more than one in four children in this country lives in poverty. Part of the problem is a modern blurring of what constitutes a family.

Some modern changes in the meaning of family were for the better and were long overdue. John Locke in the seventeenth century had said that the abuse of the monarchy as a paternalism might have been avoided with a single change of language: "If we had realized that this supposed absolute power over children had been called parental, and thereby discovered that it belonged to the mother too." It took almost another three centuries before Locke's proposal of the verb "to parent" came into use.

Parenting does not have to be a monolithic process. There are occasions when father and mother make contrasting contributions to the parenting process. And the reverse is true in the way children contribute to the lives of their parents. Eliot Daley makes the interesting suggestion that we still lack the verb "to child." That is, just as each father and mother parents the child, so also each boy and girl childs its parents. Each parent brings out something different in each child; each child brings out something different in each parent. What the parent experiences in this relation can change radically over the years. A friend said that when he first looked at his newborn son, he felt like saying: I'm omnipotent. A little later, during the terrible twos, he had the feeling: I'm helpless.

The parallel of a parenting process and a childing process should not be taken for equality. Especially with very young children, the adult's responsibility is immeasurably greater than the child's. The parent has a solemn responsibility to tell the truth to a growing child; in contrast, a child will experiment with language and often be unclear about what truth demands. A child's lying should not be condoned but nevertheless it is the capacity to lie that signals an inner life and an arrival at maturity.

The idea that children should be accorded rights is one that has taken hold in recent decades. In 1988, the United Nations promulgated the Convention on the Rights of the Child, adopted by one hundred ninety nations. The only two abstentions were Somalia and the United States. The United States is always resistant to international treaties. In this case, the conservative groups may have had a basis for their fear, insofar as the assertion of numerous children's rights (of expression, assembly, religion) could undermine family authority. The child would be liberated from parental authority but only by state intervention and control. (The other main objection to the Convention, that it forbids the execution of minors, is a less defensible, even reprehensible, argument.)

The contention that the child has a right to his or her religious beliefs seems contradicted by the U.N.'s two Covenants, one on political and civil rights, the other on economic, cultural, and social rights. Both documents assign a right to parents for the religious education of their children. The inconsistency may be due to a failure to make distinctions about the meaning of "child." The United Nations' stipulating that child means anyone under eighteen years old fails to distinguish between children before the age when they can reason, children who can use their reason but lack experience, and children who may be managing households. A child's right to his or her religious beliefs has a different meaning at age seven and age seventeen, which is not to say that the child's religious views at age seven should be disregarded.

Some rights, such as voting, should be granted earlier. Lowering the voting age from twenty-one to eighteen was not based on any principle and has done very little to engage young people politically. Lowering the voting age to twelve (or younger) would be based on the principle that one learns politics by participating in it. Children's views should be respected. They would probably make some foolish mistakes in voting (as opposed to adults?) but they could learn from their mistakes. Some rights may need greater restriction by age, such as driving an automobile. A child of sixteen does not usually have the experience and maturity for handling a potentially lethal automobile. Raising the driving age to eighteen is helpful, though it perhaps should be raised to twenty-five to avoid the daily massacre of young lives on the highways.

The political reform of family life should be one of improving the care of the very young by adults while at the same time respecting the step-by-step development of the child into young adulthood. The churches can be a major force in trying to maintain this healthy tension between adult direction and the child's impulse toward liberty.

An educational reform of family is in the direction of making it a more genuine form of community, a union of all the members while also affirming the individuality of each person. It is also part of the church's mission to be a reminder that family is not the only communal form. Roman Catholic parishes are still often described by the number of families they have. The attitude reflected in this way of speaking is not a welcome sign to people in search of a community.

It may be objected that in references to a parish consisting of families, the meaning of family is broader than a unit in which children are being raised. This objection fits well with a tendency present from the beginnings of the country, and especially strong in twentieth-century social science, to call almost any grouping a family. It is always debatable how far a metaphor should be extended, but in this case the primary meaning often seems to have disappeared. Instead of a baseball team or a law firm being compared to the primary unit of care for the next generation, the team, group, committee, or organization is simply claiming to be a place of good feelings. If every group can be called a family, the specific concern of caring for children gets lost, not of course by parents, but certainly by government officials in charge of economic policies.

Church as Communal Form

The church can have an impact on community experience by attending to the family in its relation to outside forces. As the *Catechism of the Catholic Church* says, "Family catechesis precedes, accompanies, and enriches other forms of instruction in the faith." The church has to avoid joining the rest of society in over praising and under supporting the family, which results in the individual family turning inward. A family desperately needs the help of both other families and non-familial community groups. In the past, the Catholic Church offered one alternative under the somewhat unfortunate name of "religious life" (thereby excluding most of the church from religious life). The idea was a good one, a kind of community that would challenge the limits of ordinary life, especially the economic system. The Christian Church still needs a variety of religious community forms. We seem to lack, however, the Benedict, Francis, or Teresa who might re-create religious communities for our day. The Catholic Church has been a good source of community experiments but its language here is stuck in the middle ages.

I should note, however, the growth of movements in the Catholic Church during recent decades. They signal a search for communal experience beyond family, parish, or religious order. Some of these movements are well known in the United States: Catholic Charismatic Renewal, Cursillo, and Marriage Encounter, although as a kind of replacement for the parish these movements have flourished more in other countries. They also raise liberal fears; Focolari or Communion and Liberation are criticized as too conservative. Opus Dei has achieved notoriety as a secret society suspected of wielding subversive power. Whatever one's view of a particular movement, the phenomenon bears watching as the Catholic Church tries to re-structure its forms of community. The clinging to traditional piety by these groups should not be the sole basis of their rejection by liberal reformers.

Protestantism, which affirmed the family as a more genuine religious community than the monastery, succeeded in making the point for the churches of the Reformation, but without offering substantive alternative forms. This is a place where Protestant-Catholic cooperation has to move beyond sixteenth-century reformation and counter-reformation. There are millions of young people and comparable numbers of older people who would like to be in a religious community, which they cannot find adequately expressed in an isolated family situation or in a novitiate. The Community of Taize has been an example of Protestant-Catholic cooperation in providing an experience of religious community, especially for hundreds of thousands of young people.

I am not disparaging the efforts of the local church to be a religious community. Many people do find their local church to be the chief communal support of their lives. In research that asks people which organizations are important to their life, the church in the United States ranks first, and everything else is second. The question is whether that relation to church means holding membership in a large organization or experiencing a profound communal bond. One imaginative pastoral leader can sometimes be the difference in unlocking the potential for communal expressions. Yet, intelligence, good will, energy, and imagination of people are sometimes hidden behind apparent lethargy in many local churches.

It is important that a local church not go completely on its own, that it be part of a network of regional, national, or international renewal. Some programs may fail to work but that is the way humans learn. It should also be noted that a program that lasts for five years or one year is not necessarily a failure. If there is a multiplicity of communal forms, most of them need not be permanent for the individual. The Catholic religious order wisely had annual and triennial vows, but unfortunately, it came to speak of people who did not stay permanently as defectors.

Church and Sexuality

The Christian Church has a formidable challenge in being a haven for the family and other non-familial forms of community. The standard question "Are you married or single?" reveals almost nothing about a person's life, certainly nothing about community. One might say there are two kinds of marriage today and innumerable ways of being single. The situations of the divorced and widowed do not comfortably fit anywhere in a split between married and single. Singleness can range from the sadly reclusive to the profoundly communal. Married couples who have the immediate care of children are in a very different situation than couples who do not. This same contrast applies to homosexual as well as heterosexual couples.

Young people today are exposed to a flood of sexual imagery before they can begin to figure out who they are and what they want in life. Any child who can turn on a computer can easily find material that would have put a person in prison fifty years ago. The sexual repression of the 1950s (masked in the idealized family sitcoms of the time) is not a model for today. The feminist and gay revolutions have worked changes that are irreversible. But the changes have come so rapidly and so widely that no one is sure what it all means. During the Clinton affair, children were asking their parents, or more likely someone other than their parents: what is oral sex? Many of the older generation were asking each other: what is phone sex?

At present, the government is spending a billion dollars a year on what are called "abstinence only" programs. It is puzzling to me what people mean by "teach abstinence." In practice, it seems to have two parts: telling youngsters don't do it and telling them birth control often fails. It is surely desirable that adults encourage young people to wait if not until marriage at least to the time of a serious, loving relation for sexual activity. But it is duplicitous to expect young people to abstain from sex while society is relentlessly selling them sex.

The results of this approach to sexual education are depressing: the United States has some of the highest rates in the world of sexually transmitted diseases, pregnancy, and abortion among teenagers. Worse still, teenagers who take the abstinence pledge and fail (which most understandably do) are less likely to take means to avoid pregnancies and abortion. Instead of emphasizing decision and will-control with young people, churches could be more helpful as places of communal support where young people could seek advice when they need it and find forgiveness when they fail.

The dramatic sexual changes over recent decades do not signify the end of the family or the total corruption of youth. Both fears have been themes throughout our history. Starting from the Boston synod of 1680 that bemoaned the fact that "fathers are not keeping their sons and daughters from roaming the streets at night," and "women are befuddling men with their naked necks and arms," each generation has been sure that the family has just collapsed and that today's youth are incorrigible. In the middle of the nineteenth century, Emerson quotes a friend saying, "How terrible it is for our generation who were born when adults were in charge and now when we are adults the children are in charge."

One should not, however, underestimate the difficulty of growing up in today's world; some things really have changed. It is a fact, for example, that the divorce rate has skyrocketed in recent decades (Catholics have a lower rate of divorce but one-third of marriages between Catholics end in divorce). Divorce and remarriage can lead to awkward arrangements of joint custody and stepparents. But many of the divorces are healthier choices than in the past when there was more societal pressure to remain in miserable and abusive relations. Actually, more children live in a household with one or both parents than was the case in the 1940s. One-parent families today struggle to keep together rather than dissolving the unit as commonly occurred in the past.

Homosexuality is an unavoidable issue today. Homosexual relations might be viewed as a healthy complement to family life rather than be seen as its enemy. This question is at least open to discussion today. A poll at the time of Pope John Paul II's death showed that the percentage of U.S. Catholics who did not see a problem with homosexuality was slightly higher than the rest of the population. Churches could offer a good setting to discuss homosexuality and other practices that in the past have been considered deviant.

The sexual scandals in the Catholic Church are a terrible obstacle to the credibility of the church in dealing with sexual and familial issues. Still, it is by showing some imagination, leadership, and energy in this area that it can rehabilitate its image. There is still a rich foundation of Catholic family life and a variety of communal organizations to work with. But the Catholic Church cannot reshape itself in isolation. It has to work with and learn from other churches. It has to provide realistic religious community forms within which the sexual is acknowledged, including provision of rituals for engagement and courtship.

Dialogue Within

The Christian Church is one of the few institutions that has a chance to link the outstretched hand in daily life and participation in a global institution with a mission other than financial gain. Martin Luther King, Jr. used to say, "We are tied together in the single garment of destiny, caught in an inescapable network of mutuality." The reality of that single garment can easily be lost sight of in the press of ordinary affairs, or it can be reduced to the one network of buying and selling. The church can learn from the advertising world how to attract customers but any gimmicks and techniques have to be kept subservient to another kind of mission, that of being the best example of community it can manage. Big churches may be a sign that the message is being well received, though one would have to look at other facets of the operation, especially communal characteristics. A decline in numbers can cause panic in a world obsessed with market shares, but once again other factors should be considered.

All the churches, but especially the Roman Catholic Church, now have to deal with an increase in the freedom to choose. In a pluralistic society it would be unhealthy not to imagine being outside as well as inside the community. As Robert Wuthnow says, "It (this imagining) involves comparing values of more than one community, and, indeed, recognizing homogeneity of beliefs within a particular community. This capacity permits individuals and communities to grow and to change." An individual has to consider whether the community's teachings are the same as his or her own beliefs. There is a process of negotiating differences throughout one's lifetime. While Islam says "there is no compulsion in religion," it nonetheless tries to prevent conversion away from the Muslim community. The Christian Church as well cannot enforce such conformity even if it wished to do so.

If there is real freedom to choose, there will inevitably be some people who choose to leave the church community. That does not necessarily mean the community has failed. A young person may need to get distance from his or her parents, however good and caring the parents are. The distance can make possible a new appreciation of the parents. Similarly for one's religious community, a young person may have to go around the world to discover the place he or she started from.

The church leader should not panic when someone chooses to leave the community. True, it can be a time for soul-searching about ways to improve the communal experience. But as every conscientious classroom teacher has to learn, sometimes the failure to connect is not the teacher's fault. George Hagmeier said many years ago, "Sometimes all one can do for young people is stand on the steps of the church and wave good-bye. But do so with a smile on your face; they might be back."

Local churches should consider occasionally offering programs for ex-members, that is, church members who were scared away, drifted away, or were put off by ecclesiastical scandals. Things can look different five or twenty-five years later. There could be a series of talks and discussions with the clear understanding that a person's attending does not signal a commitment beyond the four or six week series. Churches on university campuses are often in a good position to offer an intellectually challenging program to people who are curious but disgruntled. If no new "converts" result, there can still be value in the outreach and results may not show until months or years later. Few people are argued back into a community; one thinks of Cardinal Newman's "I want to deal with inquirers not controversialists." But intellectual seriousness is important within a larger context of genuine friendliness, openness, and caring.

A realistic form of community contains three generations and two genders. A test of community is whether there are helpful exchanges between the genders and among the generations. Every relation between boy and girl, man and woman, doesn't have to be immediately and overtly sexual. A church can be a relatively safe place to work out friendships that may or may not lead in the direction of sexual relations. The absence of friendships in the lives of middle-aged men is a stark reality. As discussed above, adolescents today are in an almost impossible situation in navigating their way to sexual maturity. But the middle-aged, whether single, married, divorced, or widowed, can be just as confused. Even old people (old is whatever your age is plus twenty) can be in search of help, companionship, or sex, and they do not have many places where they can sort out what they are looking for.

Providing community experience for the older generation is an obvious ministry for churches. Many churches do have widow/widower groups for people grieving the death of their spouses. Beyond that, churches can provide a meaningful role for the old who often feel useless after their families are grown and they are retired from a salaried job. I have noted the importance of the relation between grandparents and grandchildren, one of the largely unexplored educational experiences. When this relation does not exist for older people, churches can develop a program of adoptive grandparents that provides a role for older people (and some relief for harried parents).

The relation of old and young applies not only to infants and young children but to adolescents as well. If the setting is right, the older person and the teenager can find common cause; they are both outsiders to a world obsessed with rational productivity. Nursing homes can use the presence of both young children and adolescents. Done with care, the relation can be beneficial to both ends of the age spectrum. The youth minister in a church has to remember that all programs don't have to be aimed at service to the teenager. The young may have untapped good will and energy which could use an outlet.

Some teenagers who are rebelling against their parents need another set of parents, at least temporarily. That may sound like a wild new idea but what is relatively new and fairly wild is the assumption that two parents (or even one) can supply all the guidance and care that is needed to grow up. In the seventeenth-century colonies, a boy at age twelve was apprenticed to another family. In addition to learning a trade, he in effect received a new set of parents. An interesting twist on that practice is that girls also went to a new family even though they were not learning a trade. The African phrase "It take a village to raise a child" has unfortunately become a cliché of political infighting. More than a village and less than a village go into educating the next generation, but any institution that can provide moments if not years of safe, affordable, responsible help is a first step.

The two great educational moments are being born and dying. For the person at the center of each process, it is the transformation of human existence that is at stake. For the community members who are in the closest circle around the star performer, it is also a transforming time. For the Christian churches, birth and death are the two great challenges locally and globally as to whether the church is a living organism, dying and being reborn daily. There are innumerable committees, workshops, and seminars that a church may wish to offer, but it is concerning birth, death, and rebirth where it should be expert.

The larger society still has some sense of ritual surrounding birth. Prenatal care, baby showers, birth announcements, and instructions for new parents are often available for the middle class. At the end of the nineteenth century the advent of the obstetrician to replace the midwife brought some medical advances but often at the expense of the human aspects of the process. Women have recently made progress in restoring a more personal touch to birth without abandoning sane medical practices.

Especially after the birth, many women need comforting and advice from other experienced mothers and fathers. The last century and a half produced a flood of books on infant care (most of them written by single men); these books were often intimidating. After Benjamin Spock's down-to-earth advice book, the manuals improved, but new parents continue to need more than books. With some imaginative organizing, the church can be a link between young parents who feel isolated with a newborn child and a whole company of unpretentious expert help.

The most obvious place for a church to offer an alternative organization is in burying the dead. There is no need to rehearse here the deficiencies of the funeral industry, its outrageous costs, and the failure of reforms. Some churches and synagogues have taken up the challenge. There are responsible funeral directors (outside the two big corporate chains) who are open to doing things differently; many of them rightly see their work as an extension of church ministry. A church can change the experience of death, starting from the moment of death, continuing at the funeral, and remaining throughout different stages of mourning. In churches where there is a Lazarus committee, a group of church members is on the scene from the beginning to give whatever assistance they can. This could include building a wooden coffin, using the church building as an alternative to a funeral home, or seeing that individuals are not exploited when they are most vulnerable.

Bringing food to a mourner's home at the time of the funeral is a fairly well-established practice. But seeing that a widow or widower is eating well three weeks or six months later is not often attended to. There is a delicate balance here between wishing to be of help and not being intrusive. Some people who could use help are very reluctant to ask. A small group from a local church is more likely to find the balance than a large and impersonal organization. The Catholic Church in particular has long-standing rituals surrounding death, which I discuss in the following chapter. It is not a big jump involving great expense to add a personal and communal touch to existing rituals.

Most local churches and certainly the global church would do well to tone down the claim of being a "community." The church is called to be a demonstration of community and, in fact, it does a better job at that than most other organizations, big and small. But the rhetoric of community is so abused and overused in the contemporary world that unless there are groups demonstrating mutual care, rhetorical claims to community are vacuous. And, lest the church's fragile experiments at the local level melt away or turn completely inward, bigger reforms of church structure are needed. Organizational reforms will not result in the Christian church being one big community, but they might help to support communal experience wherever it is found.

CHAPTER FOUR

❧

Liturgy and Work

When a community is a Christian community, one of the central patterns and rhythms it develops is a communal life of prayer, a characteristic set of forms for addressing the mystery of God.
> —Fashion Me a People, p. 94

In her usual low-key way, Maria Harris introduces the central activity of the church, the liturgy. For many people, liturgy, which means the work of the church, is puzzling. In what sense is it work? I indicated in Chapter Two that work is a universal educational value, one of the stand-ins for the purpose of all education. I also pointed out the danger of reducing work to job. Without a challenge to that reduction, human life can become a joyless search to fill up the hours on the job by making more money and to fill up the time off the job by being entertained. The work that is liturgy is not a metaphorical extension of the forty-hour week but a call to center all other forms of work within the origin of the meaning of work: "God saw everything that he had made, and indeed, it was very good" (Genesis 1:31).

Liturgical Reform

Although much still remains to be done, many churches are beginning to do the serious educational work of reshaping this particular ecclesial form, leiturgia, *with end (the search for meaning and purpose) and without end (the awareness that the worship of God is never-ending.*
> —Fashion Me a People, p. 102

Liturgy, it must be admitted, is a strange-sounding word imported directly from Greek. It is part of the church's intramural language and not much used outside of church circles. Such language can carry a wealth of special meaning, but of course, it is also subject to becoming just ecclesiastical jargon. Many Catholics have changed from "going to Mass" to "attending the liturgy," but the gain in such a change of phrase is doubtful. A continuing education for Catholics is needed to appreciate the liturgy. The problem is that the liturgy is itself supposed to be the center of that education. *The Constitution on the Sacred Liturgy* embodies the paradox when it says that the liturgy is the starting point and ending point of all that the church does. Can one get before the starting point to ask whether liturgy is well understood? I offer in this chapter some reflections on the nature of art, work, and teaching not as issues more important than the liturgy, but as insights into the preeminence of liturgy in Christian life.

Protestants are more comfortable with the word "worship"; it does not have the esoteric aura that "liturgy" may have. But the problem is equally acute in rescuing the idea of worship from the superficial assumption that everyone understands what worship is and how it is practiced. The difference between liturgy and worship can be just an historical accident—though more seems involved here.

Liturgy has connotations of an elaborate performance appealing to all the senses: the sound of bells, the sight of gold vessels, the smell of incense. The reaction of the outsider can range from a grudging admission that the Catholic Church (like the British monarchy) can put on a great show, to the scathing criticism that Catholic liturgy is nothing *but* a show. Does the spectacle overwhelm and distract from the simple center of the church at prayer? Protestant references to worship rather than liturgy concentrate on "God's word addressed to the assembly and the people saying 'Amen.'" The preaching of the word is usually joined by music in which the whole congregation joins. The church member does not attend worship as a spectator but participates in a service to God.

Here as in other areas, Catholics and Protestants have recently been learning from each other, though there remains a pronounced gap in how liturgy/worship is approached. Catholic liturgical renewal has been at its best when simplicity has functioned as a key principle. Of course, just emptying the church of clutter does not of itself produce a better prayer service. A new simplicity has to serve the performance of the liturgical rites. Unfortunately, the Catholic Church may have been short of artists when enthusiastic reformers stripped the altars bare. What was needed was better art. For example, nothing is wrong with a statue of Mary, the mother of Jesus. Devotion to the "Virgin Mother" is undeniably part of Catholic tradition and remains so in contemporary prayer. Churches open to a more artistic representation than some awful nineteenth-century statue can link that old-time religion with a present aesthetic sensibility.

Protestant churches from the other direction, without abandoning their own distinctive tradition of simplicity of worship, have picked up hints from Catholic ritual and spirituality. One can approach mystery with all of one's senses; the process does not culminate in well-formed concepts but in awe. Silence before mystery can be either mere passivity or an openness to God's grace. Reinhold Niebuhr, who had been the most famous preacher in the country, wrote an extraordinary essay when he had become in his words "a pew worshiper" rather than the preacher. He had come to think, "these pulpit-centered churches of ours, without a prominent altar, seemed insufficient." He concluded, "I came to view the Catholic Mass as in many respects, more adequate than our Protestant worship. I realized that I envied the popular Catholic Mass because that liturgy, for many, expressed the mystery which makes sense out of life always threatened by meaninglessness."

The liturgical movement dates from the beginning of the twentieth century, led by a coalition of learned monks and devoted lay people. It was not an inward-looking movement; it originated with and remained joined to biblical scholarship and the ecumenical movement. Also, it was never far removed from protest in the name of economic justice. The Catholic Church in the United States is indebted to a few dozen scholars and ordinary church members who kept alive the idea of liturgical reform in the 1940s and 1950s. The election of Pope John XXIII proved to be the surprising opening for the Spirit that issued in the Second Vatican Council. The part of the Council that had immediate impact for ordinary Catholics was liturgical change. Suddenly, Catholics throughout the world became aware that Confession, Confirmation, Mass, Extreme Unction, and numerous other rites were not fixed in their familiar forms; new names indicated a different form of prayer.

The immediate reaction, which still has echoes today, was bitter resistance in some quarters and excited endorsement of novelty among some reformers. When reformers try to make religious rituals relevant, they might assume that they understand the present era and where history is going. They have a tendency to adjust the ritual to what are superficial characteristics of the contemporary scene. But sometimes what is most relevant to the time is buried under the trivia of the present moment awaiting contact with art that has survived for centuries. Liturgy in a global church exists locally; it cannot be legislated for universally.

People who are labeled conservative are sometimes mere resisters who are nostalgically attached to whatever they once learned. Many of the people called political conservatives in the United States today do not show much love for the past or respect for ancient institutions. But conservative in religion often does mean a respect for the past, a love of the whole Christian tradition. This kind of conservative is suspicious of radical changes that are not deeply rooted in knowledge and love of the past.

Church Music

I remember being at the Liturgical Conference meeting in 1965 when for the first time the congregation lustily joined in singing "A Mighty Fortress is Our God." It was a thrilling moment in which Roman Catholics joined sixteenth- and twentieth-century Lutherans in a gesture more significant than the Catholic-Lutheran near-agreement on the doctrine of justification. But while Catholics could embrace many Protestant hymns, they still had to find their own voice, style, and rhythm.

The Second Vatican Council said that in the Roman liturgy "Gregorian chant holds pride of place." That music has a grand simplicity based on the rhythms of the Latin language. Not a music that an ordinary congregation would sing, it existed mainly in the monastery and a few church choirs. When the Council approved liturgy in the vernacular languages, Gregorian chant was promptly eclipsed. I used to tell people in the early 1970s to save their *Liber Usualis*; Gregorian chant will return. I had no idea it would come back so quickly or for a while be at the top of the popular music charts.

Gregorian chant could never be more than a small piece of the liturgical music in the contemporary Catholic Church. The principle is nonetheless important that liturgy should include a variety of forms of music, including music that has existed for centuries in

At the local church where Maria and I worshiped, the music was typical of Catholic churches: off-key mumblings of badly composed hymns. I used to nudge Maria and ask, "Why don't you go up there and stop this bleeding?" With sixteen years of choir directing and the experience of leading innumerable conferences in singing, Maria was unused talent—unused because the pastor had no interest in finding out what talents were in front of him. That pastor died (as it happens, on the same day Maria died; perhaps she led him into heaven with a song). The new man is an unpretentious fellow who sees himself as presiding before a democratic assembly that is the church. He did not have any musical training but he knew enough to tap whatever musical talent was in the parish. Sure enough, we had people who could sing. As our choir now leads the congregation each Sunday morning, I enjoy it by imagining how Maria would enjoy it.

Catholic tradition. Some of it may require a musical artist or a team of artists for its performance; some of it may require preparation by a choir; some of it should be readily accessible to an assembly that is helped out by a skilled leader. There are Catholic churches where one finds such a serious approach to music, presided over by ministers who have a degree in liturgical music. These ministers make an invaluable contribution to the church's overall ministry.

Unfortunately, music is still a neglected stepchild in most Catholic churches. The church lacked musicians in the 1960s when it suddenly decided to have different music. The music at hand was the folk song of protest accompanied by guitar. I suspect there are Catholics who found themselves at a "hootenanny Mass" in 1965 and resolved never to go to church again. I have often wondered if Vatican II had been in another decade would the results have been any better. I don't think the insipid ballads of the '50s or the hard rock of the '90s would have offered a better model for liturgical music than did Peter, Paul, and Mary. One thing sure is that liturgical music cannot be relevant to today by simply adopting the popular music of the day. MTV will do it better.

Anyone with an artistic appreciation of music is liable to get depressed at the state of music in Catholic Churches. One thinks of Friedrich Nietzsche's truculent comment that "if they wish me to believe in their savior, they will have to sing better hymns." In the long run, the Catholic Church will have to win over talent, artistry, and creativity, which are often associated with rebellious, idiosyncratic, and stubborn people. It is unclear that church leaders are ready to embrace non-conforming characters who can enrich the church with contemporary music that is also consonant with its past. In the short run, there could at least be moves in the right direction if the leader of the assembly tapped into whatever talent is present in the group.

Liturgical Action

Music is the most obvious but only one of the arts that shapes the liturgy. Every human art could conceivably find a place in Christian liturgy within which the human body at the center of creation is presented at the altar of praise and thanksgiving. Liturgy, as the public expression of the church's life, affirms in an artistic and stylized way the fundamental gestures of human life. Of course, the most intimate of human activities should not simply be exposed to public view. The activities of the bedroom and the bathroom are appropriately private, which is not to say that they should be unrecognized or denied in a sacramental religion.

The morning blessings in Judaism include thanks to God that the bodily ducts and cavities are working. At least one Christian mystic, Julian of Norwich, wrote of human elimination as sacramental, the natural correlative of eating. That may strike the contemporary reader as bizarre but much of our ecological problem reflects an inability to accept our place in the chain of consumption and elimination. All of our bodily actions, whether public or private, can be sacramental. But perhaps we need to examine whether eating should be a public act, and, if so, under what conditions.

Eating Rituals

One of the primary myths in religion is that of communion with the gods. A sacred meal is often the central act of worship. This fact does not reduce the Christian Eucharist to one of many myths. But it is not surprising that the "Lord's Supper" is at the center of Christian worship. The celebration of the Eucharist links the past events of Jesus' passion and the future eschatological banquet with the present experience of a community meal (1 Corinthians 11:25–26).

The Eucharist is a sacrament, the sacralizing of one of life's most basic and frequent actions. Eating is a reminder of human animality, a daily remembering that we are of the earth and dependent on the fruits of the earth. Like sex, eating is a pleasurable activity that transcends its obvious nutritional purpose. Also like sex, religions have surrounded eating with rules not because the activity is bad but because it is so good as to make us forget other human goods.

Christian rules for eating were one of the casualties of the sixteenth-century Reformation. Protestantism generally rejected the traditions of fasting and abstinence. Roman Catholics hung on to some of the rules until the Second Vatican Council. When I was a child, one of the clearest badges of being a Catholic was eating fish on Friday. Attempts to maintain or reform rules of fasting and abstinence seem to have been done half-heartedly and ineffectively.

Religious rules about eating do not make a lot of rational sense. That is always a strong argument against them. But that is also their point. The lack of meaning to the outsider is what unites the community who observe such rules. A community's eating rituals remind members several times daily who they are, even when they are away from the community. Anthropologist Mary Douglas criticized Catholic Church leaders for trying to substitute love of neighbor for Friday abstinence. Douglas's judgment was that "the liturgical signal boxes were manned by color-blind signalmen."

Contemporary Christians may look bemusedly on Muslim, Jewish, or Buddhist dietary laws, but perhaps Christians have to look at both their own early tradition and at contemporary confusions around food and drink. The fourth-century writer Evagrius of Pontus, famous for his enumeration of the seven capital sins, called gluttony "the mother of lust" and "the terror of moral purpose." In our day, the misuse of food takes many forms; overeating and anorexia, a taste for foods that are produced only with extreme pain for animals, absurd amounts of money spent on foods harmful to health, binge drinking by college students who have not learned how to drink alcohol. The United States is the world's chief example of a people luxuriating in a surplus of food but not using their riches wisely.

When I walk across Penn Station at any hour of day or night and meet hundreds of people eating and drinking on the run (literally), I wonder if the nation's health problems, starting with obesity, can ever be addressed without some sense of eating as sacramental. The problem is that liturgy in church needs a base in the practices of family, household, and small community. Judith Martin, under the name of Miss Manners, has a good sense of the indispensability of ritual for human civilization. Of the importance of family and household meals she writes: "A household where the members do not sit down at dinner together nearly every night is a convenience store, not a home."

So much of contemporary politics and economics conspires against good and healthy habits of eating but much of the problem lies in attitude. The work schedules, especially of poor people, may make the family meal seem like a romantic fantasy. But the rich, with less excuse, have eating habits as bad as those of the poor. There is no point in forcing unbending schedules on people. Still, it is the nature of ritual to shape people's habits. For civilized human beings, it is important how food is grown, cooked, and eaten. I think as a general rule no one should preside at the eucharistic liturgy who does not regularly prepare meals for other people.

Religious concern with food and with eating properly may seem out of place in a world where a billion people go hungry. But if one understands eating as a sacramental activity, one would be impelled to a concern with food for the starving. There is a time for fasting and a time for enjoying good food and good drink with friends. When a wealthy Jew told the Maggid of Mezeritsch that he lived on bread and salt, the rebbe ordered him to eat cake and drink wine. "If you are content with black bread and water, you will come to the conclusion that the poor can subsist on stones and spring water. If you eat cake, you will give them bread."

The Ritual of Dancing

Unlike the steps of a ladder or a staircase, the steps of our lives are much better imagined as steps in a dance, where there is movement backward and forward, turn and return, bending and bowing, circling and spiraling, and no need to finish or move on to the next step, except in our own good time and God's. —Dance of the Spirit, p. xi

One of Maria Harris's favorite metaphors is dance. She insisted that the stages of development were not to be imagined as steps up a staircase but as steps in a dance. She agreed with Tom Driver that "all the temporal arts, including narrative, are descended from dance, which is built upon our bodies' rhythms in time and space." The liturgy as a whole is an elaborately choreographed dance of the community with God and before God.

Dance is the highly-stylized way that liturgy acknowledges the other fundamental activity of human life: sex. We share with the other animals organs of reproduction but as far back as can be traced, humans have made an elaborate dance out of this bodily function. Not surprisingly, an activity that is passionately involving and the source of intense pleasure is also the source of suffering, exploitation of others, and self-destruction. Every religion puts constraints on sexual expression not because sex is evil but for its own good. Sometimes religions, including Christianity, forget that all the rules are to govern what is good, not oppose what is evil.

Once when I was teaching a course on mysticism, I invited a rabbi friend to speak on Jewish attitudes and practice. In his talk, he said that sexual intercourse is a sacred act that brings married partners closer to God. A Thai monk in the course vigorously objected on the grounds that sex is a great distraction and can be a main obstacle to enlightenment. As I stood listening to their intense disagreement, I thought they were actually not so far apart. The orthodox rabbi knew very well that sex can be an obstacle and needs rules, while the Buddhist monk did not think that sex is evil.

The church's public worship cannot include sexual relations in its most overt expressions. But sex is not equivalent to sexual intercourse. Sexual play reaches down to every playful gesture connected with self-discovery and intimacy with others. Sigmund Freud scandalized many people by pointing out the discovery of sexual pleasure by infants. For adolescents, concern with sex can overwhelm all other interests. Insofar as actions throughout life are directed toward fulfillment and unity, the sexual is ever present. It is sometimes claimed that religious activity is sublimated sex, but it could also be said, possibly with more truth, that sex is sublimated religion. That is, sexual intimacy comes closest to fulfilling our religious longings. Precisely for that reason it can become idolatrous and be mistaken as the solution in the mystical search for oneness.

The liturgy should be a highly-stylized play of sexual movement. The president of the assembly gets to do most of the moving, while outfitted in pretty garments. Each gesture is choreographed: where and when to walk, how to extend hands and fingers, when to break into song, when to be breathlessly quiet. In the Catholic missal, the choreography was called rubrics, the part printed in red. A good dancer knows how to follow choreography not as a robotic control but as a helpful framework within which to communicate with the audience.

Of course, the community of worshipers should not be a mere audience of listeners. Although listening is not necessarily passive, the community's role has to include more than listening. The whole community, not just the presider, needs to move. Prayer is movement of heart and soul, mind and body. The movement of the body in the liturgy was largely reduced to sit, stand, kneel, and for some, approach the communion rail. Fortunately, the procession on special occasions never died out, especially at marriages and funerals. Processions are a simple form of dance; the introduction of a small procession at the offering of the gifts was a helpful addition to the eucharistic liturgy.

The re-introduction of the kiss of peace in the Eucharist was one of the best reforms of the liturgy. Kissing can range from a fairly innocuous greeting to a deeply erotic part of sexual relations. The liturgy quite properly includes the kiss in a highly restrained form. Nevertheless, it is a gesture that allows a friendly exchange and a real kiss with intimates but also, in Rilke's phrase, the "circumspection of gesture" with strangers.

Young children particularly like the kiss of peace; it appeals to their irrepressible bodiliness and their sense of play. Children, in fact, are a good test of whether the body is being respected in the liturgy. If children are screaming, they might be just having a bad day or else they may be doing what many of the adults feel like doing. The most joyous, adult liturgies I have ever experienced have been ones that provided an integral place for infants and small children. Yes, it can get a little messy, but that's a good reminder of what life is like. Liturgy is serious but not solemn.

A full-scale reintroduction of sacred dance into Christian liturgy seems unlikely. The dancers were driven from the temple early in Christian history; they were judged to be too frightening and not needed. Perhaps if the music were really stirring, some simple dance movement would emerge (and in some cultures it does). The performance of a dance by a trained dancer can be an appropriate element on occasions. Like music, everyone does not have to do everything.

Because it involves the whole Catholic community, the Rite of Christian Initiation of Adults is a model for catechizing the whole community. The adult who is entering the church journeys toward the reception of baptism in the context and with the support of the parish community. Even when the one baptized is an infant, the community can be involved in the preparation for the event, the liturgical experience of the baptism, and the follow up through reflection on its significance. The experience of baptism should be tied in with the liturgical calendar; most fittingly, it is administered during Holy Week services. If done at other times of the year, it should still be accompanied by several weeks of public ritual that convey the serious nature of what is beginning.

Liturgical Form

The theme of this chapter is the liturgy itself as educational form, that is, the liturgy is the teacher. Because of the narrow meanings of teach, teacher, and teaching that dominate modern discourse, one might take the claim that the liturgy teaches to be a figure of speech, a metaphor based on what everyone knows a real teacher is. Christian Church leaders can be taken in by the rationalistic and individualistic meaning of teaching rather than the expansive and profound understanding of teaching that is manifest in religious history. In a sacramental view, as Thomas Aquinas said, everything and everyone can teach. But as Mary Douglas writes, the education of church leaders is likely to prevent them from understanding community, symbol, and gesture as educational.

The *General Directory for Catechesis* says that the "liturgy must be regarded as an eminent kind of catechesis." That is a profound insight that must be correlated with an adequate meaning of teaching. The liturgy teaches by being what it is, the community performing a public ritual that expresses all dimensions of human life. Liturgical performance can be viewed as one aspect of the catechizing of the Christian in how to live out a gospel-centered life. Parts of the liturgy may be directly instructional. The sermon is a different kind of teaching from most of the liturgy. As I will describe in the following chapter, the sermon should be very directive, not a folksy chat. But the rest of the liturgy is not a sermon in disguise.

When it is assumed that teaching consists of someone explaining a subject, usually at the front of a classroom, everything other than rational discourse is seen as mere instrument. Poetry is then taken to be just a contrived form of prose, and stories are assumed to be nothing but containers of lessons. Anything other than words is thought to be just atmosphere for telling people what is so. But when genuine liturgy is placed at the center of religion we are reminded that from infancy we are taught in a myriad of ways. Rational explanation is at best a clarifying of what we have already experienced. Most teaching is done by a community. When any individual steps to the center and arrogates the title of teacher, the obvious question is: Who appointed you? A teacher who does not have the authority of a community is highly suspect. A teacher's words have to draw from the life of a community. A community does most of its teaching nonverbally. Members of the community learn by living within the group and absorbing its views and postures. Rodney Stark once defined conversion as "coming to see the world the way your friends do," not bad as a sociological description of conversion. We are taught by example, both good and bad. The individual teacher does not give examples so much as is an example. The teacher for the most part is unaware of teaching; teaching is often more effective when it is not intended. Karl Barth wrote of Mozart: "He does not try to teach but simply plays, and it is as such that he teaches us that creation praises its Master."

Great artists usually understand that their art teaches, but not in the form of rational explanation. Catherine Madsen notes, "Art must rough up the perceptions in order to restore the capacity for sustained attention." Guardians of orthodoxy who want art that does not upset anyone because it recites banalities are an obstacle to a living liturgy. The musician cannot be instructed to write only uplifting lyrics; the sculptor cannot be restricted to pretty statues. Music, painting, sculpture are good teachers when they have an integrity to their composition. Good art is likely to draw the response: What is that supposed to mean?

Public, Personal, Private Prayer

From the time of the ancient Greeks, "public" and "private" have been defined in opposition to each other. For the Greeks, the public was the place of the light of truth, where free persons lived. Private was the negation of the public; it was to be de-prived of public space. It was the sphere of women, children, and slaves. In the secular revolutions of the eighteenth century, especially in the newly born republic in North America, there was a near reversal in the meanings of public and private even though women, children, and slaves did not noticeably benefit. Privacy became the valued sphere, the household providing protection against the intrusion of the public. The meaning of public is dominated by the government and a threat of oppression. The saying "private wealth, public squalor" is not new in the United States. Anything with public in its name (housing, toilets, transportation, school, television) is likely to be under-appreciated and under-funded.

The Christian liturgy cannot flourish on either side of this dichotomy: valuing the public at the expense of the private or settling into the private sphere by neglecting what is public. The family is too private; the government is not public enough. To the extent that the church is a community of persons it offers an alternative. The person is the meeting place of public and private; they can be seen not as separate spheres but dimensions of human activity. Liturgy is not public prayer as opposed to private prayer but rather a prayer that with a face turned toward all creation can also include the most profound inwardness of a person. Liturgy has to be experienced as a work that transcends individual hands while it allows inward feelings of joy, anger, sorrow, doubt, and grief. No individual is clever enough to be able to invent such ritual; it is the work of generations.

Funerals and Mourning

A ritual of mourning is probably the oldest human ritual. It is also the biggest challenge today for relating public and private. In modern times, burial and mourning became almost completely privatized, that is, located in a hidden sphere without a public ritual. A study of grief in the 1960s by Geoffrey Gorer found that only Orthodox Jews and Roman Catholics seem to have anything near to an adequate way to deal with death and mourning.

Starting with the political assassinations in the 1960s, the country has seemed to acquire a taste for public expressions of grief and plenty of talk about death. At least when a celebrity dies or when a terrorist strikes there are public displays of pictures, notes, flowers, and the ever-present television camera. Some television talk shows are mostly composed of very public, sometimes embarrassing, expressions of grief. The embarrassment a viewer can feel is for people expressing themselves before a camera and studio audience in a desperate effort to find a community of mourners. The attempt is not likely to succeed. But while televised confessing and forgiving, grieving and comforting, are easy to mock, people use whatever rituals are available and whatever sense of community they can muster.

Despite the splashes of public grief when a celebrity dies, the ordinary person may still lack any of the ritual that nearly all cultures have had for burial and grief. The contemporary funeral may be a series of speeches, praising the deceased. A little humor at such a serious moment can be helpful relief. However, the ideal seems to have taken hold that a funeral is a time to try out a comedy routine. Without traditional ritual to sustain private grief, people toss about for the right words and the appropriate tone. The comforter should not have to come up with brilliant new phrases. A traditional formula or silent interstices in the ritual should be ready at hand.

When I was growing up, I knew almost nothing about Jewish practice. I did know that the Jews buried their dead within twenty-four hours, which seemed to me cold and inhuman compared to the Irish wake. I knew nothing about the sitting of Shiva for seven days following the burial (a kind of wake after the funeral) or the elaborate ritual from the moment of death through the subsequent year. When I did study Jewish rituals, what most struck me were the many parallels between Jewish and Catholic practice. Christians would do well on this point as on so many others to study Jewish practice, if only to better understand their own Christianity. Jewish ritual was not designed for psychological comfort; the tradition says the ritual is a command to be fulfilled, not a support for a psychological need. But the ritual does help the mourner's private grief; it achieves that in being public work.

When the Catholic Church revised its funeral liturgy, I was skeptical about its being an improvement. I was accustomed to the unrelieved starkness of the funeral Mass and the frightening boom of the *Dies Irae*. I did not want a priest telling me that we should all feel happy, that we should celebrate the resurrection and not feel bad about the death. I was not won over until 1981, when at my father's funeral I experienced that the ritual could provide for a range of feelings. The ritual largely carries itself, but it allows places for individual variations. Of course, in the Catholic Church one still needs a cooperative attitude on the part of the priest. For my father's funeral the priest was open to suggestions from my sister and me. The funeral was designed so that all of the family, including the youngest grandchildren, had a part. The ritual comforted, a word that means to bring strength. We had feared, for example, that my mother would just collapse at the funeral, having been so dependent on my father through fifty-three years of marriage. My mother had had trouble walking for many years but the funeral ritual proved to be supportive. I remember her practically striding down the center aisle as fifty nuns led the church in singing.

Over the last quarter century, I have been at more funerals than I can count. I have seen funeral services that were mechanical and depressing, but I don't think the fault lies with the ritual. Sometimes it is just that conditions of modern life interfere with the performance of any serious ritual. For example, the ride to the cemetery can be a harrowing experience in New York. The big cemeteries on Long Island always seem hours away from the church, amid highways with seventy-five miles-an-hour traffic. That is not the kind of procession which best serves the ritual. On that point, I particularly remember the funeral of Frederick Schaeffer, a close friend of Maria's and one of the best priests I have ever met. The whole church walked in procession out the door and into the cemetery behind the church. The after-burial meal was on the church grounds at the edge of the cemetery. There was good reason for the traditional practice of the cemetery being in the churchyard.

Liturgy and Professional Work

Liturgy is a peculiar form of work; at least it seems peculiar in a culture that thinks of work in instrumental terms rather than as an ultimate value. People go to work to make a living. At its worst, the job is boring or burdensome, made bearable by the salary check and the summer vacation. At its best, work that is professional is valued because it is experienced as worth doing. One receives money but there are more important things in life than piling up money. Leisure, a centering of the soul, is intrinsic to work. The professional is fortunate enough to have a job that is real work and is leisurely. Unless health problems interfere, one need never retire from such work; teachers, priests, and prophets have a life's vocation. Professional work has to resist being swallowed by a market system in which value corresponds to price tag, where nothing is valued for itself. In the genuine meaning of professional, a person does not become professional by a licensing board saying so.

In New York City, I often feel there are now two kinds of workers: those who are bored out of their skulls and going through the motions, and those who really care about the quality of their work.

Some of the people being paid big salaries and called professionals are in the first group; some people bagging at the supermarket, cleaning trash from the streets, and washing windows belong to the second group. John Kultgen has proposed doing away with the noun profession as a sociological category, but at the same time extending the adjective professional to any work well done. My first reaction was that the suggestion lacks logic and is too paradoxical. But I have come to think that he is right and we need to praise work well done as professional while improving the shape of jobs that serve all of us without worrying about whether a particular job is called a profession.

Liturgy is a community praising, thanking, and petitioning God because the work is worth doing. Its form encourages private sentiments but it does not depend on the capacity of individuals to generate such sentiments. It is simply there—there in history, there in place, there before and around us. It does not immediately express one's immediate feelings. On a day that I feel joyful, the morning prayer may begin, "Out of the depths I cry to thee"; or the reverse can happen: I can be faced with a hymn of joy when I am grieving. But the singing of a psalm can lift me from an overly introverted attitude and link my feelings to a worldwide religious body and generations that have gone before me.

Catholic tradition includes a peculiar sacramental doctrine: belief in *ex opere operato*, meaning the work is effective simply by the work having been performed. These days that belief can be a source of embarrassment, but the doctrine goes to the nature of sacraments. The doctrine may seem to express a magical attitude toward the sacraments, and historically, that is often what happened. Come into the church and look at the host; your life will be changed. Recite your sins to the priest and all will be forgiven.

One individual's holiness or lack thereof does not make invalid what is publicly expressed. A central aspect of the *ex opere operato* doctrine was that God's grace is not dependent on the holiness or disposition of the minister. The doctrine is a denial that the priest is a middleman between God and the laity. Priests do not forgive sins; priests do not make Christ present. God, in conjunction with the faith of the church, makes such things happen.

Such a belief could be an excuse for sloppy, mechanical performance on the part of the minister and a magical attitude on the part of the congregation. But anyone who appreciates the ritual will perform it to the best of his or her ability. Any artist or true professional does the work to the best of their ability and then does not claim credit for the achievement. Let the work speak for itself. Any great performer knows that he or she can coast through a performance and most people probably will not notice. But a performance of Hamlet, the Marriage of Figaro, or the Eucharist deserves the respect due to a great work. The Christian believes that this work is the culmination of creation.

Private Prayer

Private prayer is often thought to be completely different from liturgy, even in opposition to it. But the private in private prayer as the interiority of every human activity is at the core of all liturgy and worship. The Christian who prays in the quiet of her room or when riding the subway can still be linked to the church's liturgical life. Private prayer is a centering of all life in relation to God and creation.

Private prayer can be both verbal and nonverbal. It is a peculiar kind of conversation because God does not do any speaking, at least in any words that most of us recognize. (As the cynical joke puts it, "When we speak to God it's called prayer; when God speaks to us it's called schizophrenia.") When the other party is not holding up his or her side of the conversation, we are inclined to fill the empty airtime with nervous chatter. The exception is when we are with someone we have known and loved for years. Then two people can comfortably sit in silence for long stretches of time. Silent presence can communicate volumes.

There is nothing wrong with words in prayer, especially the recitation of ancient texts and traditional formulas. When Jesus was asked, "Teach us to pray," he responded: "When you pray, say: Father, hallowed be your name" (Luke 11:2). He did not invent a new prayer. Each of the phrases of the Lord's Prayer is taken from the writings of Jesus' Jewish people. God has heard it all before, so there is not much point in trying to be completely original.

What can seem bizarre to the outsider is the rapid repetition of formulas that sounds mindless. An old woman "telling her beads" or a choir of monks rattling through a litany do not seem to be paying any attention to what they are saying. The words are said too fast to allow for any reflection on their meaning. A person reading the New Testament on the subway might be trying to find an inspiring message to get through the day, but repeating the name of Jesus with each step may seem to be on the edge of madness. Prayer, public or private, that is said in an emotionless tone can indicate either a lack of feeling or else a highly compressed and deeply reserved emotion.

Constant repetition of a prayer is one way for a person to find the center of the soul. A common image in the history of religions is a turning wheel. We find ourselves whirling about our daily affairs, never able to fix our gaze on the big picture. We can seek a place of rest in one of two ways. Either we can try to get away from it all ("Stop the world, I want to get off"), or we can go toward the middle of the wheel. At the exact center of the moving wheel is perfect stillness. The mystic finds the still point of a turning world through silence and the rhythmic repetition of prayer.

In a related image, at the eye of a hurricane there is an astounding calm before one gets hit with the backside of the storm. Daily life is more like the hurricane than the wheel in that one knows the calm is soon to be followed by swirling winds. The repetition of prayer formulas is like a protective barrier expanding if only temporarily the blue sky in the hurricane's eye.

Prayer formulas and other bodily gestures surround the still point at the center of the soul. Karl Rahner once wrote, "The Christian of the future will be a mystic, or he or she will not exist at all." That sounds like an extreme demand, given what people associate with mysticism. But mystic, meaning silence and union, is not found only in the desert and the monastery. (Thomas Merton thought the future of the monastery is in the urban center.) All prayer that is profoundly private has a mystical simplicity to it. The mystic is "oned with God." Christians follow in the footsteps of the person they believe to be perfectly oned with God.

Several prominent theologians of the twentieth century posited a direct contradiction between revelation and mysticism: either follow the road laid out by the Scriptures or adopt a claim of direct access to divine union. There is no denying that mystical claims have often created tension and sometimes outright conflict with church doctrine. But a meaning of revelation that cannot include the mystical needs to be re-examined. The Christian Scriptures are for the Christian the unparalleled verbal expression of divine revelation but cannot be equated with that revelation. If one starts with "Christian revelation," a phrase invented in the late sixteenth century, one is liable to mistake revelation for an object under church control. If one begins with a divine revelation that the Christian Church interprets but never controls, mystical experience is not excluded.

Church leaders have often seen a conflict between mysticism and sacraments. A mystic, such as the fourteenth-century Meister Eckhart, has often been taken to be a misplaced Buddhist, who bypassed ecclesiastical channels for his own unorthodox way. Eckhart was misunderstood in his own time and condemned by church officials; in Thomas Merton's words, "He was a great man pulled down by a lot of little men." Most writing on mysticism takes Buddhism as the primary example, and as a result Christian mystics do not quite measure up. But perhaps a liturgical, sacramental, Christ-centered mysticism is another route to oneness rather than a competitor with the Buddhist path. Jewish and Christian prayer practices find their own way to the still point in a turning world.

For Maria Harris, the best image of this center is the Sabbath. Maria did not develop this idea in *Fashion Me a People* but it was a theme that ran throughout all of her writing. In *Jubilee Time*, she wrote, "Sabbath is primary ground in the ritual of Hallowing, just as it is the fundamental pause, stop, and no-saying in Western spirituality" (p. 35). I could never fully grasp why the image of Sabbath occupied the place it did for her, but it was at the center of her writing on women's spirituality, economic justice, and interreligious dialogue.

Sabbath is a multi-layered symbol at the heart of Jewish practice and education. It is a beautiful reminder to both Jew and Gentile that at the center of busyness there has to be a place where work and leisure are united in the delight of doing nothing. The biblical account of creation appears to have an inconsistency. It says that God finished the work on the seventh day; it also says that God rested on the seventh day. The rabbis debated whether creation took six days or seven. The rabbis' solution was that creation took seven days; it was on the seventh day that God created his greatest gift: the Sabbath day of rest. Thus, in Jewish practice, "for six days we struggle to endure and repair the disaster around us, on the seventh day we eat and sing and make love."

Paradoxically, this day of rest is also a symbol of the fight against injustice. The land and the animals are also allowed to rest (Deuteronomy 5:15). The poor are remembered as being in need of food and clothes. Regarding the Sabbath, Nehemiah says to the Jews returned from Babylonia: "This day is holy to the Lord your God....Go your way, eat the fat and drink sweet wine and send portions of them to those for whom nothing is prepared" (Nehemiah 8:9–10).

The Puritans to their credit took seriously the command to sanctify the Sabbath but they misunderstood the spirit of festival. Their grim enforcement of Sunday laws led only to rejection of any controls. The result is that Sunday eventually became a day for shopping and football. Against the pressures of secular culture, Jews do better than Christians in their Sabbath observance. Sunday is still a day off from labor for most people. It is church-going day for many Christians. Other than that, it is often difficult to find a Sabbath attitude in the Christian observance of the first and eighth day of the week, the day of creation and re-creation.

Sabbath is a weekly observance, one day in seven. It also applies to one year in seven—the sabbatical leave. College professors (who already have a rather leisurely life) are one of the few groups that get sabbatical leaves to refresh their work. Maria was especially fascinated by the Sabbath of Sabbaths, the fiftieth year. "You shall hallow the fiftieth year and you shall proclaim liberty throughout the land to all its inhabitants. It shall be a jubilee for you" (Leviticus 25:10). Maria often spoke to groups of women about celebration and reflection during their fiftieth year. The idea of Sabbath becomes the center point of jubilee spirituality for the second half of life.

Catholic tradition kept alive the idea of jubilee years, a special time of forgiveness and peace. The Catholic Church declared the year 2000 a jubilee year and it was joined by many other religious and secular groups. It was a year that called for the forgiving of debts which poor countries owed to the rich. During the years leading up to 2000, Maria's was a strong voice in this movement that did have some success. Her own work as a speaker and writer came to an end in the jubilee year, but her work and quiet presence continued.

CHAPTER FIVE

Proclamation
and Witness

Kerygma *has always been taken to mean both what is proclaimed and the act of proclaiming. For Christians, the proclamation is the life, death, and resurrection of Jesus, the Christ; of a saving God whose word is with and for the people being fashioned.*
—Fashion Me a People, p. 127

Maria Harris begins her chapter on *kerygma* as an educational ministry by giving this comprehensive picture of the Christian message and how it is delivered to the people who are the church. The present chapter and the one that follows are about forms of teaching that are mainly verbal. They are extensions of the liturgy or elements within the liturgy. This chapter is especially concerned with preaching which finds its best setting in a liturgical context. The chapter that follows this one examines Christian teaching mainly in a context of secular education and interreligious dialogue.

In my treatment, I have reversed Maria's two chapters on *didache* and *kerygma*. The two topics are intimately connected and their order is not of crucial importance. In the way I understand their relation, an initial proclamation of the gospel is followed by moral guidance, intellectual reflection, and adaptation to local conditions. The *kerygma* or announcement comes first; *didache* or detailed instruction comes second. I do not know why Maria chose a reversal of that order. My guess is that she wanted to make an immediate connection between the gospel message and the call to service in the chapter that follows these two chapters in *Fashion Me a People*. And it is quite possible to take *kerygma* as summing up the whole of what church ministry is about.

I remember the first time during a course in 1956 that I heard about something called the "*kerygmatic* approach" to the teaching of religion. I was curious but I found the discussion esoteric, mostly the insistent work of a few enthusiasts. Coming mainly from missionary centers, this new approach did not seem to be startlingly different and its educational method seemed simplistic. The teacher was to recount the story of Jesus' life, death, and resurrection backed up by the history of salvation in the Christian Old Testament. The expectation was that students would brighten up and respond enthusiastically. To a considerable extent that is what happened, at least for a while. The new textbooks and the enthusiasm of teachers was a big improvement over the deadening catechism that had been the staple of religion courses.

I think it was unfortunate that *kerygmatic* was first presented as a classroom approach. It encouraged many classroom instructors to become preachers, a danger that was already endemic in the role. All classroom teachers have the temptation to act the way that Hollywood movies usually portray great schoolteachers—waxing eloquent in sermons to rapt audiences of students. Teachers of morality or religion are pushed even further in that direction than other schoolteachers. I will have more to say in the next chapter about classroom teaching. In this chapter, I am concerned with preaching the gospel, which is better done almost anywhere else than in the classroom.

The most basic form in which the gospel is communicated is by the way Christians live. As Francis of Assisi said, "Preach the gospel always—if necessary, use words." Community and liturgy first made present the message of the gospel. In the church's early history the compilation of the New Testament emerged from the community celebrations of the liturgy. The first announcement, "He is risen," quickly demanded a back-story. A narrative of the passion, the sufferings, and the death of Jesus, made up the immediate narrative. Gradually, stories and sayings of Jesus were gathered together by and from trusted disciples. Some people had begun to worry that as the first generation of apostles and disciples died, many of the stories and sayings would be forgotten. A more systematic arrangement of the details of Jesus' death and resurrection, along with stories about his public life and his teachings, were put together.

I think it is ironic that Islam refers to Christianity as a "religion of the book." Some Christians today seem to agree. Actually, Christianity began as a kind of anti-book. Its story was composed not in literary Greek but in the coarse, spoken Greek of the time. Christianity is most assuredly a religion of the word but it created the book, which is what Bible means, almost inadvertently. The Christian story came together with a beginning provided by the Hebrew Scriptures. Then with the late addition of the Apocalypse or Revelation of John, an ending was provided for the book. Revelation was the term used to describe the whole process of divine-human encounter and the story that the Bible tells. But for many Christians, revelation refers to how the book turns out in the Book of Revelation. Careful study of the Bible is unnecessary if you can find the answer by turning to the last few pages of the book. With a beginning, middle and end, the Bible can appear to fit neatly between book covers and be tucked into the dresser in motel rooms.

The sixteenth-century Reformation was concerned with returning the Christian Church to proclaiming and announcing. Christianity is a religion to be spoken, not just written about and read. The printing press was initially Luther's good friend. The word of God could not be kept secret; the word went out to lay and clergy alike. Luther, however, could not have envisioned the complete revolution that the printing press initiated. It made the word of God universally available in cheap reprint. But the danger then became that the word of God would become the words of God, that the truth was now available in book form. Luther did not intend to have each person sitting at home reading a Bible. The word of God exists as it is preached and as it is heard in the gathering of the assembly. The other Reformers were just as insistent as Luther that the church is, in the words of Luther, a mouth house not a pen house. In his German Catechism of 1536, John Calvin wrote that "the proper mark by which rightly to discern the church of Jesus Christ is that his holy gospel be purely and faithfully preached, proclaimed, heard, and kept, and that his sacraments be properly administered."

The adoption of the term "revelation" by the early church had some serious drawbacks. It is a visual metaphor—the unveiling of the truth. That metaphor has always been in some tension or conflict with the spoken word at the heart of Christianity. Revelation only became a commonly-used term when it could be identified with the printed page, a book that could be looked at and read or put away for later perusal. A typical phrase such as "the revealed word of God" does not make much sense. God did not reveal words; God revealed God through inspired words in the past and through words spoken today.

Emphasis on the present proclamation, far from disparaging the past, means that the past has not disappeared behind our backs. The past is in the depths of the present and made alive in today's narration. Past generations and the words they spoke are preserved in the memory of the community. In a book about memory in the Jewish community, Joseph Yerushalayim writes, "Meaning flowed above all through two channels: ritual and recital….Israel is told only that it must be a kingdom of priests and a holy people; nowhere is it suggested that it become a nation of historians." It would be foolish to dismiss the work of historians, and Yerushalayim as an historian is not suggesting that. But neither Jewish nor Christian religions are historical curiosities, of interest only as a book written in the past. One does not need a Ph.D. in history to tell the Christian story.

I will comment here on three languages of teaching that make up a rhetorical family of languages: storytelling, preaching, and lecturing. There are differences among these three, but they are joined in that each of them has an end in view and words are used by a single speaker to direct the listener toward that end. Such a use of language can be authoritarian and oppressive unless the conditions are right for its proper use. Teaching with these languages is not morally neutral. A degree of trust is needed on the part of the listener if the words are to work their intended effect. Trust can be exploited which is why a community has to validate the credentials of the appointed or ordained teacher.

Storytelling

The simplest and most indirect form of proclamation is storytelling. The typical storytelling community is a family or a small circle of friends. The same stories may be told year in and year out; the punch line has been heard before but it can still generate laughs. There are professional storytellers who work on a stage or who write novels and short stories. They succeed only if they build up the trust of their listeners, convincing their audience that their stories touch a human chord. Stories work best when their moral is not pushed upon the audience. A good storyteller is smart enough to let the audience draw out moral implications for itself. In this way storytelling differs from preaching; no novelist, movie director, or stand-up comic wishes to be called preachy.

Some people seem to be born storytellers; their conversation is peppered with story elements. They can hold the attention of a room with almost any yarn they spin. As in much of life, what appears to be innate has been built up over years of practice. Undoubtedly, the talent for storytelling is not equally shared but a person can develop whatever talent he or she has. "We know a poet by the fact that he makes us poets," said Samuel Coleridge. We respond to a good storyteller by learning to tell good stories.

We associate telling stories with childhood. A child picks up the rhythm of a story and is able to follow while not knowing what all the words mean. The child demands that the story be told again and again to the chagrin of the adult who may find repetition boring. In appreciating repeated story lines the child may be more in tune with the cycles of the universe. As G. K. Chesterton wrote, "It is possible that God says every morning 'Do it again' to the sun; and every evening 'Do it again' to the moon."

A storyteller risks the accusation of being childish and not facing up to the real world. The superb storyteller, Flannery O'Connor, wrote, "There is a certain embarrassment about being a storyteller in these times when stories are considered not quite as satisfying as statements and statements not quite as satisfying as statistics; but in the long run, a people is known, not by its statements or its statistics, but by the stories it tells." Storytelling can never really disappear, but it can take a form that we don't immediately recognize. If one compares an ancient tribe telling stories around a campfire with a contemporary group watching a TV soap opera, one might wonder if the human race is making progress.

Television, now joined with the Internet, has become our chief purveyor of stories. Whether situation comedies, police dramas, sports, or competition tests, television shows are successful if they are good stories. Even the news programs can compete for attention only by using story lines. That sounds fine except for the fact that the medium is so dominated by economics. A desire for profit does not destroy the possibility of telling a good story, but the point of a story to delight in providing insight into the human condition can be undermined if making money is the primary motive of the storyteller. One can bemoan the general quality of Hollywood's image machine, but at least the abundance of material means that good stories are available for someone who is choosy.

It is easy to ridicule another person's taste in stories, although maybe there should be serious concern for a culture that seems addicted to sporting events, Hollywood gossip, and movies that blow up things. A good storyteller appreciates the complexity and resources of language, even if the subject is mundane. Some of the best reporting and most imaginative use of language in the newspaper is on the sports page. The writer has to be imaginative in writing for a reader who most likely knows already which team won the game and what the score was. The story has to brim with detail; getting to the end quickly is not the point. The end does have importance but the way you get there is also important, as any writer of a police procedural knows. George Orwell wrote of Charles Dickens: "The outstanding, unmistakable mark of Dickens' writing is the *unnecessary detail*. He is all fragments, all details—rotten architecture, but wonderful gargoyles."

This point about a story's details is supported in a book by Ken Bain, *What the Best College Teachers Do*. The study found that one thing that characterizes effective teachers is how they tell a story. Good teachers take their time and flesh out the details in the story. They are confident that the audience will stay with them even though there may seem to be a waste of time in the step-by-step telling of the story. The unsuccessful teacher slides quickly over the details, anxious to make the point before losing the audience's attention.

When Maria and I team-taught, she would tell long stories, rich in detail. I was skeptical at first; I thought the audience would get restless. After enough times seeing her hold an audience, I had to admit she was right. She taught me to slow down while teaching; as Wittgenstein said of philosophy, it takes great effort to go slowly. And as Rousseau cautioned about teaching young children, one must know how to lose time. Rousseau thought that after age twelve the principle is reversed and no time should be lost. I would agree that there are times and places where instruction should be right to the point, but we are never too old for stories that are well developed and well told.

It should not be surprising that most great religious founders were storytellers. But many of their followers and their leaders keep trying to turn narratives into statements of fact. The problem is especially acute in Christianity whose founder was one of the world's great storytellers. The parables of Jesus are recognized even by non-Christians as literary gems, stories that are just as powerful today after having been repeated tens of thousands of times. Many Christians resist the idea that narratives can be revelatory; they want "revealed truths." The reason is not difficult to guess. A parable requires our own thinking about a story that has multiple layers of interpretation. In reaction the story is stripped of its details and ambiguity so that teaching can be equated with telling the truth; just the facts, please.

W.H. Auden wrote: "There are books which are only for adults, because their comprehension presupposes adult experiences, but there are no good books which are only for children." Great children's authors, such as J.K. Rowling, write stories that also engage adults. Authors who try to write down to a child's level usually produce stories that are trite and condescending.

Young children do not always differentiate fact from fiction; a good story is a good story. Many adults assume that the difference between fact and fiction is obvious. When a book presents fiction as fact there are liable to be scandals and lawsuits. There is, indeed, such a thing as lying, deliberately pretending something happened although it did not. Nevertheless, great stories often blur the line. The question about a good story, "Is it true?" most likely has the answer, "The factual details do not correspond to what an historian would find to be true but the story is revelatory of the truth."

If there had never been a Moses or a Jesus, the story of the Bible would be essentially different. As for the existence of Jonah, Noah, or Adam, that is another matter. Some people are resistant to any such distinctions; either the Bible is true or it is not. But unless one can believe (in contradiction to overwhelming evidence) that the Bible was dictated by God, one has to accept a human process of compiling stories that have a variety of forms and purposes.

The last 150 years of biblical scholarship have helped to sort out differences between fanciful stories and accounts that have an historical basis. The task is much more difficult with the Christian Old Testament stretching back before the advent of writing. The New Testament is more intent on rooting its story in fact, but even here there is a variety of literary forms: good news, letters, and apocalyptic vision. None of the New Testament is straight historical reporting as the modern era has conceived it. But in the twenty-first century we are no longer certain that one picture from one perspective shows what is real, or that stripped-down factual prose is the best way to say how things really are.

Like any good Jewish storyteller, Jesus' teaching is filled with enigmatic sayings and parables. Jewish humor is highly ironic, that is, saying one thing while you give a sly hint that you mean something else, sometimes the opposite. The tone of voice or a physical gesture is often crucial to the humor so we tend to miss what humor there is in the New Testament.

Little children are not ironic. They take language at its face value. They answer questions while assuming a literal meaning and their answers can produce unintended humor. In contrast, a grown-up ought to be able to look at the world one way and then nearly in an opposite way. A grown-up's religion has to include ironic humor to deal with life's surprises, sorrows, and disappointments. One cannot do that without some facility in the use of language. The number of years of schooling does not determine one's love of language and one's ability to play its chords. "Jesus knew and spoke out of the comic irony, which dictates that only *in* language is language conquered, only *by* language is language humbled, and only *from* language is language transcended."

Preaching

As anyone knows who has ever tried to do it, preaching is a difficult art to practice. One thing that makes it difficult is that everyone feels free to criticize this particular art. Beyond the skill of the individual preacher and the quality of particular sermons, our culture tends to ridicule or attack the very idea of preaching. Few people use the terms preaching and sermon positively, let alone enthusiastically. Yet, can there be a Christianity without the preaching of the gospel? I don't think so.

I confess to once having been among the critics who attacked the very idea of preaching. Like most Catholics, I had regularly suffered through some of the worst examples of the form. However, I had also occasionally been present when a preacher seemed to deeply move a whole audience. I was forced to confront the fact that perhaps there could be something to it. The resolution of my problem was to conclude that instead of opposing teaching and preaching, preaching can be understood as one unusual form of teaching.

Since teaching is not held in such high regard within the culture, preaching does not get a sterling new reputation by its association with teaching. Nevertheless, there is a mutual benefit for both words in this association. What can be said of classroom instruction as a form of teaching can be said of preaching, namely, it is a very peculiar form of teaching that needs the right conditions or else should be avoided. When I started writing about the positive possibilities of preaching, some of my friends thought I had had a bad conversion. The Christian church is not likely to change society's bad mouthing of preaching but it has to persist in the ministry of preaching.

One way to defend church sermons is to point out that preachers and sermons are everywhere. What can corrupt the form of preaching is the failure to acknowledge that one is doing it. Consider the minimum elements of a sermon: a speaker, words, an assumption of beliefs, and a stylized attempt to stir the hearers into action. With that meaning of preaching, it is evident that most of today's sermons are not given in church but are on television. During "the break for our sponsors," the viewer is subjected to a barrage of sermons.

In the early days of television, one went to the church of Chevrolet, Disney, or Texaco, who delivered a few one-minute sermons in the course of an hour. People may actually have listened. Today's television viewers increasingly use the mute button to avoid the string of thirty-second commercials every ten minutes. Millions of dollars are spent on these commercials, which the preaching corporation repeatedly hammers home. If you buy this toothpaste or diet pill or beer, your life will be just about perfect. The advertisers assume a community that is ripe for the product and open to the sermon. For everyone who is in the beer-drinking community, "This Bud's for you." If you are not in the beer-drinking community, the sermon can be boring or offensive.

The other place in the culture where sermons are omnipresent is in the halls of government. Politicians are speakers; that's the nature of politics. When John Mitchell, Attorney General under Richard Nixon, famously said, "Watch what we do, not what we say," he was shockingly denying the political vocation, which is to engage in the action of speaking. An effective politician is a good preacher, using words to stir a community to action. A politician has to assume belief in some texts, such as the United States Constitution, the decisions of the Supreme Court, the rules of the Senate, or the platform of the party.

The political speaker tries to get action on the basis of such beliefs, convincing an audience that the action is implied in the beliefs. We have very few great political speakers today; the reasons are many but one reason is that politicians sense they are preaching and are embarrassed by the role. Nothing makes for bad sermons like a preacher who is trying to avoid seeming to preach.

In Flannery O'Connor's *Wise Blood*, the main character keeps denying to himself and to anyone who will listen that he is a preacher. He ends up as an inversion of a Christian preacher ("I preach the church without Christ, where the blind don't see, and the lame don't walk and what's dead stays that way."). The best political sermons in the United States have usually been given by speakers who incorporate biblical sentiments into their speaking and who have a sense of justice that is compatible with the best in Jewish and Christian traditions. Martin Luther King, Jr.'s speeches are a good example of preaching based on the U.S. Constitution that echo a biblical call for justice. The tone of King's sermons is quite different from recent preaching that too intimately joins the Bible to what passes for patriotism.

Perhaps the greatest sermon ever given by a U.S. politician is Abraham Lincoln's Second Inaugural Address. The challenge he offered to his countrymen in that speech is shocking. He asks: If God has sent this war as a woe due to both North and South, can we deny that God is being just? We are paying for 150 years of the "bondman's unrequited toil" and if we should lose all our wealth, one must say as was said three thousand years ago "the judgments of the Lord are true and righteous altogether." Lincoln's speech has none of the sentiments that so thoroughly corrupt political and religious speeches in the midst of war: God is on our side and therefore we should invoke divine blessings on the young men we send out to kill.

One possibility, then, why preaching generally has a bad name is because the culture is addicted to bad examples of preaching. We say we hate preaching, but the culture is awash in all kinds of slick snake-oil salesmen who now sell politics on the basis of poll numbers. (Lincoln's numbers were not good.) No doubt there are good sermons being preached every day but they are not glitzy enough to get much attention. If the 260 words of Lincoln's Gettysburg Address had been given in today's media climate, would it get more than one minute's coverage on CBS news, the program that precedes *Entertainment Tonight*?

Putting preachers of the Christian gospel on television is generally a bad idea. Fulton Sheen could do it in the naive early days of television; the tapes of his sermons are still on cable. They show a shrewd performer delivering a well-prepared sermon. But it is difficult to imagine him having the eight o'clock Tuesday slot on a network today. Television as a visual medium is not the most appropriate place for Christian preaching. Radio is less expensive and makes more sense if one is trying to emphasize the words and not the performer. Franklin Roosevelt, Winston Churchill, and (alas) Adolf Hitler were dynamic radio preachers who would not have gone anywhere on television—not pretty enough.

When Jimmy Lee Swaggert was the most famous preacher in the country, taking in a hundred and fifty million dollars a year, I used to watch him religiously on Sunday nights. The performance was impressive. But when he would make an impassioned plea for money for his "ministry" (that is, speaking on television), I would say to my television screen: "Jimmy, if you were on radio, you wouldn't need all that money." Mr. Swaggert, like several other Christian televangelists, was brought back to earth by scandal. In his case, a bigger scandal than his being caught with a prostitute in a Florida motel room was the prostitution of the form of preaching. The unmistakable message I received from his preaching was not to get up and transform the world in the direction of the kingdom of God. Instead, it was that the problems of our world are caused by those other people (Catholics, Jews, blacks, gays, feminists). But if you will say, "Jesus is my Lord and Savior," you will be saved. The new generation of Christian preachers on television have learned to avoid some of the mistakes of their flashy predecessors, but I am still skeptical. We need good discussions of religion on television but a thirty or forty-five minute preaching of the gospel on television is a doubtful proposition.

If we turn from television to the pulpit of the local church, we find a different kind of conflict. The conflict inheres in the words *kerygma* and proclamation. The church preacher is asked to announce the good news. But is this news new? Is today's preacher, as were the apostles, facing an audience who need to be converted to the Christian path, or is the man or woman in the pulpit speaking to people who are already Christian and may be knowledgeable about the gospel? Is the saying correct that "one should not preach to the converted," or is it precisely the converted one should preach to? That is not a trick question. It goes to the heart of what the person in the pulpit can and should presume and what the purpose of the sermon is in today's Christian churches.

The gospel, and its core the *kerygma*, was first preached to people for whom the message was genuinely new. "You haven't heard this before: He is risen from the dead." Jesus says in Matthew 28 that he will return before the disciples announced this news to all the nations on earth. There are still places where the Christian message has not been spoken, and there are huge nations, such as China and Japan, where the church is a barely visible (though important) presence. The missionary is still the forward edge of the Christian movement. These days the missionary is less likely to be accompanied by an army than to be risking his or her life in a war-torn zone.

The whole church can draw inspiration from missionary work. However, there are fundamental differences between the missionary's work in breaking new ground and the work of the preacher in the pulpit or the teacher in the classroom. I said at the beginning of this chapter that the *kerygmatic* movement in the Catholic Church tried to transpose missionary preaching of the gospel to the Catholic schools of Europe and North America. The novelty in the classroom quickly evaporated. However, the *kerygmatic* inspiration has a closer relation to the pulpit.

The church sermon can be successful only if the preacher realistically accepts the limits of the form. The "proclamation of the gospel" is carried out wherever Christians provide good example to Christian and non-Christian colleagues. A person who is not a Christian is not likely to take a first step toward conversion by going to a church service. Nonetheless, the Sunday assembly should be a place where everyone is welcome. "Whoever you are and whatever you have done, you are welcome here."

A typical Sunday sermon is addressed to an audience that consists mostly of church members and perhaps a few visitors and inquirers. Most of the listeners already know the main story of the New Testament and profess belief in its message. The preacher has the simple but not easy task to draw out the implications of those beliefs with a careful crafting of words. If there are visitors actually present, they might not completely understand the sermon but neither should they find it offensive or insulting. A good sermon draws upon the intimate language of the community and may not be immediately intelligible to an outsider.

At the invitation of the congregation's rabbi, I once attended a Sabbath service in which a sermon was given by the leading Talmudist scholar in the world. I feared I would not understand a word he said. But he actually preached in simple terms on the theme "What is a Jew?" None of it was offensive to me as a Christian and I could easily understand his words although they struck home with a different impact on the rest of the congregation. Since then, I often imagine myself as a non-Christian at the time of a church sermon and try to figure out what the impression would be.

The Catholic priest should have an easier time than the Protestant minister because the expectations are lower. Catholic priests might profit from occasionally attending Protestant services and listening to the preaching. Unfortunately, preaching in Catholic churches has not improved much since the Council legislated a sermon at every Sunday Eucharist. I would have preferred a prior emphasis upon the preparation of preachers.

Flannery O'Connor tells of her cousin's husband becoming a Catholic, much to the surprise of his family. "We asked how he got interested and his answer was that the sermons were so horrible, he knew there must be something else there to make the people come." That story might be taken to be a good argument for bad sermons, but many people get driven away by disgracefully inept preaching. A priest need not fit the mold of a great orator with poetic phrases tripping off the tongue. A few minutes of reflection on one of the day's texts, spoken clearly to the audience in clean prose, should not be out of the reach of any minister.

Brevity is the soul of preaching as well as wit, though what constitutes a short sermon varies according to setting and culture. Mark Twain's saying that "few sinners are saved after the first twenty minutes of a sermon" might be a beginning. There are times when a twenty-minute sermon would be just the right length, though not usually within the Catholic Mass. Some of my African American students were shocked at a book of mine, which suggested a eucharistic sermon of five minutes or less. I had to agree with them that my proposal might be very inappropriate for their churches. I once unwisely accepted an invitation to preach in a African American Baptist Church. I gave it my best and the audience was polite but I was too far out of my element.

A preacher has to know the audience and the cultural context to judge how long to go on. The depressing fact in Catholic churches is that the rule seems to be, the worse the sermon, the longer it goes.

When a speaker sees the eyes in the audience rolling skyward, the temptation is to try to salvage the speech by saying a little more. The Hasidic master, Maggid of Mezeritsch, said, "When you deliver an address stop before the end, before you have said it all. A good speaker is one with his words; the moment he hears himself speak, he must conclude."

Length, of course, is not the chief issue, just a symptom. Appropriate length is tied to what one is trying to accomplish. I have said that the usual preacher in a church service is not announcing the gospel to an audience unfamiliar with it. The aim is not a conversion to Christianity but a small conversion of the daily kind for Christians struggling along in their lives. How about one helpful idea delivered with style? It need not be a theatrical performance but it should be forceful. The gospel, Dean Inge said, is not advice or the telling of facts; it is a proclaiming done with enthusiasm. Meister Eckhart said, "To him who hears me, I wish him well but I would have preached at the collection box." An obvious danger resides in such a forceful speaking but the task is to inspire to action.

Preaching in some form is probably as old as the human race. Could any parent get along without an occasional one-minute sermon? But it was the Christian Church that developed the sermon as an art form. At times in Christian history people could be engaged by a three or four hour sermon. Those days, it seems safe to say, are gone forever.

John Chrysostom ("golden mouth") is one of the most famous preachers in Christian history. I am suspicious of him not only because of his vitriolic anti-Jewishness but because he says of his preaching, "What greater disgrace than to walk from the pulpit with blank silence." Applause in a church may sometimes be fine, but a preacher in the pulpit looking for applause should look elsewhere. The point is not glory for the preacher but getting people up from the pew and on their way to live the gospel. An ancient historian said, "When Cicero finished speaking, the people said: 'How well he spoke.' When Demosthenese finished speaking they said, 'Let us march.'"

The time is ripe for a new leadership in using words lovingly, clearly, and briefly. In the Catholic liturgy, the five minutes after the gospel reading should be a well-crafted, quietly reflective comment on the relation of Christian belief and daily life. A good ending for the sermon would be to pose a question that asks the hearers to reflect throughout the week on the significance of the reading in their personal experience.

If possible, there would then be some kind of follow-up exercise during the week where the questions and the responses of individuals can be summarized. During the 1960s, there was experimentation with "dialogue sermons" that never went far; it is the nature of the sermon to be spoken by one person. Its effect, nonetheless, should be dialogical, indicated by the preacher concluding with a question.

It should not be forgotten that the whole service is the proclamation, which includes the nonverbal ritual, the music, the greeting of parishioners at the door, the welcoming of visitors. Protestant churches already incorporate some of those welcoming gestures, but Protestant services could use more ritual and quiet time to take some pressure off the preaching of the sermon. Dialing down the tone and length of the sermon need not mean devaluing it.

Preachers ought to be encouraged to develop their own style and not be boxed in by the stereotype of what a sermon is. Plain speech was the Puritan motto, not a bad reminder for our over-hyped era of extravagant claims. Let the message speak for itself without the preacher getting in the way. Franz Rosenzweig in his great work, *Star of Redemption*, wrote: "The prophet does not mediate between God and man, he does not receive revelation in order to pass it on; rather the voice of God sounds directly from within him." Clever manipulation by a master showman is not what the church needs now. The intelligence of the hearers deserves respect. Jonathan Edwards is unfortunately famous for one of his sermons on God dangling souls over hellfire. That does not convey what Edwards did as a preacher. Edwards "sought to convince the mind rather than to stir the emotions" and was genuinely surprised at the display of religious affections.

Preaching may seem at the furthest remove from the mystical experience of private prayer. And yet, like the other sacraments and sacramentals, good preaching brings language to its limits and issues in silent contemplation. Meister Eckhart's mysticism is found not in his Latin treatises but in his vernacular sermons (which we have access to because diligent nuns were copyists). Sermons really only exist as they are spoken; a written sermon is a pale copy. But even reading Eckhart's sermons today one can understand why he was considered dangerous, not because he was confusing the "little ones" but because his dazzling language demanding justice for the poor pushed beyond all the trite and complacent talk about a being called God. A.M. Haas writes of Eckhart: "Again and again 'God' must be spoken in order that the realm of the silent experience of the 'Godhead' be able to open us. Godhead emerges at the limits of what can be said."

Lecturing

In concluding this chapter, I mention briefly another form of teaching. Lecturing is the third example in the family of rhetorical languages, those that have a definite end in view and use a language of persuasion directed toward that end. Storytelling is a prelude to preaching; a good preacher is familiar with storytelling and uses some elements of it. On the other side of preaching, lecture follows upon preaching, drawing less on imagination and emotion while it aims at intellectual conviction. The lines that separate storytelling and preaching, preaching and lecturing, can at times be blurred. But while a preacher might be pleased to be called a storyteller, most contemporary lecturers would be offended to be called preachers.

Lecturing goes back many centuries, but it took a turn for the worse in the late nineteenth century. The word "lecture" means to read, and human teaching naturally includes reading. In the Middle Ages, church and university teaching had three operations: reading, disputation, and preaching. The first, reading or lecturing, is what a teacher did with the "sacred page" of the Bible and previous commentaries. The lecture was a prelude to disputation in which one debated with opponents about one's reading and commentary. The preaching of the word was the final operation. The thirteenth-century urban university could be a wildly disputatious place. One pope wrote to the faculty at the University of Paris to tell them to be less argumentative; they were not in charge of church teaching, he was.

The modern meaning of lecture emerged as the secularization of Christian preaching. The reading of the Bible and the commentaries, as well as debate on the interpretation, were eliminated. They were replaced by reliance on scientific fact and philosophical reasoning. The model of the teacher became the scientific expert whose authority depends on hard facts and abstract reason. Lecturing was now equated with the "expert" reading his conclusions to an audience. Alasdair McIntyre notes: "The audience came to hear and to learn from authoritative, encyclopedic pronouncements, not to dispute." Deference on the part of the audience was one of the defining marks of the late nineteenth century. This new, comprehensive lecture entered the university where it has been lodged ever since.

Like preaching, lecturing can be a valuable form of teaching when the conditions are just right. And like preaching, the last place lecturing belongs is in the classroom. Lecturing sometimes seeps down from university to other schools, but elementary and secondary school teachers could not survive by relying on the lecture. The university professor's self-image as expert in a discipline, joined with the university administration's interest in economy of scale, created the university's addiction to the lecture. The lecturer reads from a script or from notes; the students copy down what is said in case it has to be repeated on an exam.

Lecturing, as it is found in today's universities, is not much help to the proclamation of the gospel. However, reading and commentary will always have a place in Christian teaching. There is no returning to the Middle Ages, but church teachers might join with other lecturers to restore what lecture can mean and relocate its place. For example, it can be stirring to hear a poet read from his or her work. The lecturer's role is not to supply information (the library and Internet are available for that), but to show us how to shape the language lovingly.

Lectures make no sense unless the speaker has spent hours in preparing what is read. The concept of speechwriter is a preposterous invention of the twentieth century that produces cynicism in an audience. Can anyone imagine a Lincoln team of speechwriters assembling the Gettysburg Address? Fortunately, church teachers cannot afford the speechwriters that presidents, governors, and CEOs routinely employ.

If someone is going to compose a lecture of forty or fifty minutes, it requires time and thought. No one can do that every day or even every week. We ought not to be asking bishops, college presidents, mayors, and school superintendents to be always giving speeches. Let them do their jobs. A lecture ought to be a special occasion done with great attention to form. The lecturer could then say: I have spent months reading on this issue and have given the matter many hours of quiet reflection. Here in a systematic way is my best thinking in the form of lecture. Whether the lecturer reads the words or uses notes, the words emerge from his or her intimate union with the lecture's words.

This kind of lecturing has a small but important part in the church's educational ministry. At workshops, seminars, and conferences some fine lecturing occurs. The best lecturing, however, depends for its effectiveness on the readiness of the listeners. Some people go to conferences as a substitute for reading; they are looking for help in the wrong place. The lecturer is not there for supplying knowledge, which is readily accessible in writing. The lecturer's task is to mull over with the audience a shared knowledge. Their shares are not equal; presumably the lecturer has more time for reading, wider experience of the subject, and more facility at speaking before an assembly. Nonetheless, the lecturer has to count on the members of the audience being rational, knowledgeable, and appreciative of the spoken word.

Maria Harris was a wonderful lecturer, as I think anyone who ever heard her would agree. In a classroom she did not lecture; there she carried on a conversation. But she was in great demand for conferences and workshops. I heard her speak more than a hundred times at such meetings and she never failed to be carefully prepared. The person and her words were one.

The lecture is a restricted form of teaching, but the effect can be mysteriously powerful. The reason for that effectiveness, Cardinal Newman suggests, is: "Persons influence us, voices melt us, looks subdue us, deeds inflame us. Many a man will live and die upon a dogma; no man will be a martyr for a conclusion." In a world that proliferates in vacuous speeches, we still hunger for individuals to stand up and give witness to the truth as they know it, grounded in wisdom greater than their own.

CHAPTER SIX

Teachings and Doctrine

Teaching is not only initiation into the church's life, and handing on the tradition, it is not only the application and explication of the Scripture. Teaching is also the act of reinterpreting, questioning, analyzing, and even at times rejecting and resisting. —Fashion Me a People, p. 116

Maria Harris's chapter on *didache* is about teaching. That is the standard way to translate this biblical word. However, all five of these chapters on the educational forms of church ministry concern teaching. The specific character of *didache* is that it includes teachings as well as teaching. The initial proclamation of *kerygma* was naturally followed by interpretations and commentaries. Each generation has had to work out applications for new times and new places. Occasionally, course corrections have been in order.

The first generation of Christians could not have imagined how complicated the process would become in the course of thousands of years. *Didache* in the New Testament refers mainly to immediate follow up, that is, the moral implications for the first followers of Jesus. The teachings are found in the scriptural canon and in subsequent writings that provide guidance for living according to the gospel's teachings. In this chapter, I comment on the nature of this process for establishing what is acceptable and what is unacceptable in the Christian life. Then I will discuss the dialogue of Christian teaching with other religions and the formation of Christians to live in today's world. Dialogue with other religions of the world is thought by some Christians to be contrary to the Bible and a dilution of faith. Admittedly, the New Testament does not foresee such dialogue and it is a challenge to some Christian teachings. But avoiding the question, with its possibilities as well as its dangers, is not educationally responsible.

Dialogue between traditions, such as Buddhist and Christian, or Jewish and Christian, presupposes dialogue within a tradition. In that sense the interreligious dialogue that was seriously undertaken only in the twentieth century is an extension of a dialogic attitude, which runs throughout the tradition. Such an attitude is more evident in Jewish than in Christian history. One reason for Christians to study Judaism is to gain appreciation for the fact that disagreement need not destroy the tradition. In Christianity's continuing relation to Jewish tradition, the Christians until recently did all the talking because they talked only with (dead) Jews in the Old Testament. It has been a great step forward in the last half-century for Christians and living Jews to talk about their agreements and disagreements. Such cooperation has, among other things, thrown light on the origins of Christianity.

Despite the New Testament's negative picture of the Pharisees (reflective of church-synagogue conflict), Jesus' teaching was similar to the Pharisees. It was the Pharisees who taught that God is a loving Father who would not abandon any of his children, that each person is responsible before the judgment seat of God, that death is conquered by resurrection. The Pharisaic reform, several centuries before the Common Era, introduced the very idea of tradition. Instead of directly taking on priestly authority and its control of sacred texts, the Pharisees introduced the idea of a second source, what has been handed down orally.

Tradition provided liberation but it also had its dangers. Sacred texts can be restrictive and lead to narrow-mindedness but they also are a restraint on officials. Tradition has no such controls when the claim is made that secrets have been whispered from mouth to ear. What saves tradition is that it eventually gets written down before it again breaks out orally. Commentaries on commentaries make tradition not an entirely separate source but the interpretive context of the sacred writings.

The existence of this traditioning process implies a continuing interpretation, debate, and disagreement within the tradition. The Talmud says: "Moses pleaded with the Lord to reveal the final truth in each problem of doctrine and law." The Lord replied: 'There are no pre-existent final truths in doctrine or law. The truth is the considered judgments of the majority of authoritative interpreters in every generation."

That attitude may seem to conflict with the idea that God has revealed the truth, a fixed and final truth. It is more accurate to think that God initiated a dialogue, which, if genuine, involves response on both ends and an arguing for one's case. As Job found out, the humans and God are not equal but that does not automatically end the argument. In his "Commentary on the Book of Job," Thomas Aquinas asks whether Job should have been arguing with God. Aquinas's very Jewish answer is: If you are sure you are right, keep arguing even if it is with God.

The life, death, and resurrection of Jesus introduced a radical change in the Jewish tradition from which he came. But this profound shift was not a rejection of the tradition. In Christian belief, Jesus is the culmination of divine-human encounter. The Christ figure does not terminate the process but instead becomes its interpretive key. The dialogue of God and "his people" continues.

Jesus as the Christ is the fullness of revelation but we are still thrown back on words not only for individual belief but also for the church's teaching as a whole. Neither the New Testament nor any subsequent doctrine can be the revelation of God. The New Testament teaching is the best witness that Christianity has: "This is what we have heard and this is what we have seen." From the very start the witnessing was diverse and filled with potential conflicts of interpretation.

Doctrinal Teachings

I noted in the previous chapter that the gospel accounts emerged out of the liturgy. As it became apparent that the Christian movement was in for a long haul between Jesus' resurrection and the resurrection of the whole Christ, a written record became imperative. Three versions of the gospel developed, each guaranteed by a witness to the resurrection. It has always amazed me that the early church did not try to get its story straight by lining up one version. These days a marketing specialist would probably advise that three versions of one story (and eventually a fourth that strikingly differs from the other three) is not good strategy. How can you convince the world that you have the final key to human history when you cannot even decide which report to choose?

The early church teachers had some flexibility because they did not mistake their words for God's. They had to engage in discussion and debate to decide which teachings give authentic witness to the revelation of Christ (Paul recounts some intense verbal jousting). It has always been known that there were writings that claimed first-hand knowledge but did not make the cut. Some of these writings have been discovered only in the past century and others may yet surface. While these other documents can illuminate the church's beginning, the church has no inclination to reopen the biblical canon.

Presumably, the decision about which books to include and which books to exclude involved political debate and compromise. The fourth gospel, attributed to John, was admitted to the canon in a balance with the First Letter of John. The Gospel of John's emphasis that love is more important than any commandment had led to some unruly Christian communities. The First Letter of John goes straight to the issue: "Now by this we may be sure that we know him, if we obey his commandments" (2:3). A longer controversy about inclusion in the canon concerned the last book of the New Testament. The *Revelation* of John was long disputed before it was finally accepted for the canon.

Revelation ends with Christ but Christ has not ended. Christians believe that the New Testament is divinely inspired literature but it is literature nonetheless. The documents express belief and are the primary witnesses to beliefs that need continuing debate and reform. It is sometimes inaccurately said that there is a "deposit of revelation" fixed with the death of the last apostle. The phrase with the longer history is *depositum fidei* or deposit of faith. The difference is profound. What the apostles bequeathed to future generations are testimonies of faith not revealed truths. Thomas Aquinas always refers to doctrine as based on "articles of faith" not articles of revelation.

The formation of doctrines continues to require the church "overseers" to listen to the past and to the present in trying to find expressions for what is ultimately inexpressible. A teaching that is called a dogma is the least inadequate expression that the tradition has been able to formulate. And as Meister Eckhart pointed out, the dogma may leave out more than it includes.

When I tell non-Catholics that my church has over 2000 defined dogmas, they usually ask: Do you believe all of them? To which I reply: I don't disbelieve any of them. Some of them make no sense to me but I don't spend my time railing against one doctrine or another. To judge any one doctrine, it has to be related to the whole body of Christian teaching. A doctrine that is now unintelligible to me may make more sense at another time and in another place. The body of Christian teachings is to me a brilliant kaleidoscope of language that invites further thought.

A doctrine of the church is true within the body of Christian truth. As Christian language, "Jesus is Lord" is true; outside a Christian context, the statement is neither true nor false. Christian doctrine becomes meaningful for an outsider as Christians live by the truth of their statements. An outsider can get inside enough to perceive meaning and the possible truth of a doctrine, but as George Lindbeck notes, "The Crusader's cry 'Christus est Dominus' is false when used to authorize cleaving the skull of the infidel."

In 1950, Pope Pius XII declared as a dogma of the Catholic Church that Mary the Mother of Jesus was assumed bodily into heaven. The pope's action set off a firestorm: voices of dismay from some Catholic scholars and cries of betrayal from many Protestants. After threatening to set back by decades Catholic-Protestant cooperation, the doctrine had the effect of forcing some rethinking about the relation of Scripture and tradition. If the assumption of Mary is nowhere "contained" in the New Testament or the first few Christian centuries, what is the relation of any official doctrine to a deposit of faith? Is "contain" a proper metaphor for any doctrine's relation to tradition? Might the Catholic Church find a wide range of untapped doctrines in its tradition?

Consider, for example, the belief in reincarnation. The Second Council of Constantinople condemned the belief as incompatible with the doctrine of resurrection. Despite that ruling, belief in reincarnation never died out among Christians. Polls today indicate that as many as one-fourth of Catholics believe in reincarnation. That fact may simply indicate ignorance of the tradition and a poor job by teachers. But could there be something here to reconsider? I am always hesitant to dismiss out of hand what a majority of the human race has consistently believed. Is it possible that the sixth-century church dismissed reincarnation prematurely? Would the doctrine actually support the meaning of resurrection for some lives? Whether or not one thinks a soul is infused at conception, there are millions of lives that seem aborted before an individual has had a chance at any semblance of personal experience.

It is possible, of course, that a child may have lived a more concentrated human existence than some adults whose lives are stuck in one recurring pattern. It is not for any of us to judge whether an individual life has been fulfilling or not, but it certainly seems that some lives are cut short. Would it not make sense that they get a second chance so that in these instances a resurrection of that life would be meaningful? Reincarnation, instead of being opposed to Christian doctrine would fill out a missing piece. I don't believe in reincarnation, but neither do I disbelieve it, at least as a possibility and in a way compatible with Christian doctrine.

Whatever a Christian teacher thinks of reincarnation's fitting within the boundaries of orthodoxy, people who hold such a belief should not be immediately read out of the church. Perhaps the Christian Churches, and Catholicism in particular, have been learning that debate and disagreement can be healthy. As Thomas Aquinas says, "We must love them both, those whose opinions we share and those who opinions we reject. For both have labored in the search for truth and both have helped in the finding of it." In this spirit, the Second Vatican Council was a great improvement over both its nineteenth-century predecessor and most church councils, which were quick to condemn heretics. Vatican II, with its theological advisors and Protestant observers, was an admission to the world that bishops, too, have to listen, learn, debate, and then decide in fallible, human situations. The Council's condemnation was wielded only once, in referring to nuclear war, the one fitting place where *anathema sit* belonged.

Moral Teachings

Teaching is not only toward knowing and understanding the Christ of the gospels, toward making this lore a part of us, it is also toward examining the implications the lore has for our own lives. It is about how we act as well as about how we think. It is toward asking and responding to the question, "What would you have me to do?"
—Fashion Me a People, pp. 111–12

More than other doctrinal issues, questions of morality were raised for every Catholic following the Second Vatican Council. Unfortunately, Catholics since the Council have found it difficult to maintain the spirit of dialogue within the church. A sharp division of attitude was perhaps inevitable as an ancient institution tried to make some dramatic alterations. Civil disagreement is part of dialogue but separation into hostile camps is not. The Catholic Church has struggled to find a common ground on which to build a consistent moral teaching.

Birth Control Controversy

Since the end of the 1960s, the Catholic Church has been riven by opposition between groups called liberal and conservative. One thing the two groups agree upon is the significance of the papal encyclical, *Humanae Vitae*, on birth control. One side sees the document as a failure to carry through on the spirit of the Council; the other side sees a failure of church authority to crack down on dissidents who rejected the document. Apparently the great majority of U.S. Catholics do not accept the moral teaching in that document, a fact that the church must somehow comes to terms with lest it lose all moral authority.

Shortly after the Council, Pope Paul VI appointed a commission to study the question of birth control and advise him. The committee was made up of tried and true Catholics who were deeply loyal to Catholic tradition. One of the few women on that commission described to me the atmosphere of conflict at the first meetings. Opinion was almost unanimous against any change in the teaching on birth control. But as a result of conversations that became civil and thoughtful, the opinion at the end of the commission's work was the reverse. All but a few members favored change.

The pope disregarded the recommendations of his own commission and reaffirmed past teaching. Many loyal Catholic scholars immediately voiced disagreement with the papal document. Given such disarray, millions of Catholics also decided on their own against the pope's teaching. The term "cafeteria Catholic" was coined to describe an attitude of picking those doctrines you like and disregarding those you don't like. Some Catholics who disagree with doctrines may have that attitude, but it is an unfair characterization of millions of others. Many loyal Catholics disagree with this teaching on birth control because they firmly believe that their own experience is more consistent with a catholic, sacramental morality than is the papal document. They could be wrong, but many Catholic priests and bishops quietly agree.

The pity is that this disagreement could have been a great teachable moment, a time to think carefully about the basis of Christian morality, a time for some devout Catholics to share their experience in a way similar to what happened within the papal commission. The Catholic Church is in a difficult position; it cannot abandon what it has tried to protect. It badly needs dialogue along with some distinctions that would open up new avenues for the moral principles it sees at stake.

It is regularly said that the Catholic Church is against artificial means of birth control but that is not accurate. The Catholic Church's opposition on principle is to whatever is opposed to the proper exercise of human powers. What is artificial can fall under that proscription but need not. Artifice is the stuff of human life. Artifice that is violently destructive deserves to be condemned (destroying the water supply, exploding bombs on a bus, kidnapping children to be soldiers). Artifice that serves human dignity and environmental integrity, such as warm clothes, solid housing, organic farming, is to be praised. The distinction holds for all the ways that the human race controls birth. The Catholic Church ought to continue condemning those artificial means that are destructive of the human body and human dignity.

The Catholic Church has traditionally been very good at making moral distinctions. An unfortunate aspect of *Humanae Vitae* was a collapsing of distinctions in the attempt to shore up its teaching on contraception. After condemning abortion as a means of birth control, it says other forms of contraception are "equally to be excluded." By placing abortion on the same plane with all other forms of birth control, it undermined the church's teaching on abortion. Despite the impassioned condemnation of abortion by Catholic bishops, U.S. Catholics do not show much difference from other citizens in their attitude to it.

The tragedy here is that the Catholic Church, despite being ridiculed for its attitude toward sex, is trying to defend the "natural powers" of the human person against promiscuity, trivialization, and violence in the name of liberation. The integrity of the human person is indeed at stake. The Encyclical says that each sexual act has to have an "openness to life," a phrase that needs an expansive rather than a cramped meaning. There are plenty of sexual practices that are doing violence to girls and boys, women and men. The Catholic Church, in conjunction with other churches, should be addressing violations of life, something it cannot credibly do while caught in its narrow bind on birth control.

End of Life

On sex, death, and other important issues, the Catholic Church has usually been defending the right principle. But if the devil is not in the details, the complexity of moral guidance in a technological world is. On "end of life" issues, the Catholic Church has had a much better reputation than it has on sexual matters. It has staunchly defended the principle that killing a patient is wrong even if done as "mercy killing." It carefully distinguished that principle from the practice of allowing a person to die. I find it astounding that as early as 1958, Pope Pius XII (not celebrated as a liberal reformer) wrote that turning off a respirator was morally allowable in some situations. The issue was barely visible then; today millions of families are confronted with it. The Catholic Church was well ahead of the curve.

The last fifty years have seen a mind-boggling increase in the complexity of medical situations. There are many cases now when the line blurs between killing and letting die. Many people dismiss the distinction as useless hair-splitting, but ethics is all about careful distinctions. As Karl Rahner said, the more complicated the moral situation, the more important it is to have a few clear principles. The United States seems to be moving inexorably toward approving physician-assisted suicide. What are urgently needed are moral principles and distinctions that are based on knowledge of complex situations. Otherwise, economics will be the one determining factor and the "right to die" will slide over into a duty to die.

Besides the medical complexity, church officials have to be aware of changes of language in addressing these issues. In the last twenty-five years the term "euthanasia" has shifted in meaning to include letting the patient die. I think it is unfortunate that secular ethicists now refer to active and passive euthanasia, which subverts the radical difference between killing and letting die. The *National Directory for Catechesis* says, "euthanasia and assisted suicide—no matter what forms they take or for what reason they are undertaken—are morally wrong." Actually, in the contemporary meaning of euthanasia, as opposed to that of a few decades ago, church tradition approves the (badly named) passive euthanasia. The Catholic Church is caught in a bind here. It can either resist the changed meaning of euthanasia or it can accept one form of euthanasia. In either case, officials have to be aware that they have a linguistic problem.

Another regrettable change of language is that the phrase "dying with dignity" has become equated with physician-assisted suicide, a terrible reduction of what the dignity of a person should mean. Dignity is one of the few terms that can link medieval and modern morality. The term dignity might seem to be an unlikely candidate on which to build a universal morality, but it has become central to both religious and secular ethics during the last sixty years.

Dignity first referred to the deference and submission due to a Roman gentleman. An upper-class individual had to be treated with respect and honor by a submissive individual in a lower class. Gradually, this idea of dignity was absorbed into Christian moral thinking not as a description of the upper class but as characterizing every human being. Meister Eckhart's "every man a king" is a paradoxical democratization of dignity. A person has dignity and is due respect simply by being a person. (Thus, dying with dignity would first refer not to what the patient possesses but what caregivers have a duty to provide.)

The treating of persons with dignity is closely associated with the concept of human rights, the main currency of international ethics. Secular ethicists cannot provide a clear explanation of why a person has human rights and should be treated with dignity. The ultimate basis, Christians would argue, is in the doctrine of creation, but the modern ethicist is skeptical about the historical record of the church on defending the rights of every person.

It is important that while the church not claim too much here (the New Testament does not talk about human rights), it still needs to be in the present conversation. Human rights will not succeed if religion is seen as an opponent; the idea of human rights has to be at least compatible with Christian and other religious traditions. When the "Universal Declaration of Human Rights" was written in 1948, religion was excluded. Eleanor Roosevelt, who shepherded the writing and approval of the document, ruled out a treatment of religion as too contentious an issue. Although excluding religion may have been a necessary expedient at that time, the question of human rights and religion has only become more urgent, complicated, and contentious over the years.

Moral Guidance

From the very beginning of Christianity, there has been a need for moral guidance. The first extant writings, such as The First Letter to the Thessalonians, are in a form of literature known as *parenesis* or direct moral instruction. Many of the writings of the Fathers of the Church have this character. Eventually, a large body of moral teachings developed, some of it having only a tenuous connection to the good news of the New Testament. This task of moral guidance is built into the nature of Christianity; the church has to develop moral positions that are consistent with its whole tradition and speak practically to contemporary situations.

The New Testament supplies the blueprint but the moral system has to be built for each age. The New Testament contains remarkably few direct moral commands, as compared for example to the Qur'an. Jesus' teaching is mainly in the form of parables and sayings that have powerful moral implications. The best-known commands of Jesus are in the collection called the Sermon on the Mount. Even here it is not clear to most people what many of these commands mean. Are calls to turn the other cheek or to go another mile with your oppressor to be taken literally? Is this a morality for all individuals? A morality for nations? Interestingly, there has been an intense movement among some Christian groups to get the Ten Commandments posted in schools and government buildings. Why not the Sermon on the Mount?

Like all great religious reformers, Jesus simplified the rules into a summary principle that he illustrated with brilliant stories. Jewish law was said to have 613 commandments. Sprinkled through the text of the Hebrew Bible are summaries that reduce these commandments to three or two. "What does the Lord require of you but to do justice, and to love kindness, and to walk humbly with your God?" (Micah 6:8). "Maintain justice, and do what is right" (Isaiah 56:1). "Seek me and live" (Amos 5:4). True to his tradition, Jesus made his own summary from existing texts; he summed up morality with the twofold command: "You shall love the Lord your God with all your heart, and with your soul, and with all your mind....You shall love your neighbor as yourself" (Matthew 22:37, 39).

There is a beautiful simplicity in this teaching that never goes out of season. As Dietrich Bonhoeffer says, "It allows the flood of life to flow freely. It lets man eat, drink, sleep, work, rest, and play. It does not interrupt him." However, over time, there did develop rules and rituals around the human activities of eating, sleeping, working, and the rest. The rules were not intended to interrupt life but that was sometimes their effect. The genuine need was for help to channel life's forces in the direction of love of God and love of neighbor.

The tricky part is finding rituals that control the small things in life so that the big things will take care of themselves. Christian moral teaching needs to have a sacramental character: the spiritual is expressed through the body. There is conflict within the human heart but there is not a conflict between body and soul. A religion of creation, incarnation, and redemption cannot be associated with a hatred of the body and human appetites. But we find it difficult to accept ourselves as good in relation to God and our neighbor.

A widespread assumption in contemporary writing is that morality, including Christian morality, is based on altruism, a word invented in the 1850s. Altruism, as the opposite of selfishness, means acting for the good of the other. Christianity is sometimes praised for its altruistic ideals and then promptly dismissed as impractical. It should be noted that morality had been discussed for centuries before any talk of altruism. Jewish and Christian morality does not say love your neighbor instead of yourself. It realistically says love your neighbor as yourself; it also says that that won't happen unless there is love for God and from God.

In an effort to control inner conflicts and undisciplined human appetites, ascetical practices have sometimes led to hatred of God-given faculties and a violent repression of them. Better the medieval saying: "Beyond a wholesome discipline, be gentle with yourself." One of my favorite lines from Thomas Aquinas is: "If not drinking wine makes you sad, then not drinking wine is a sin." Except for some blind spots about sex, Aquinas' moral teaching is profoundly sacramental. Seminary curricula that were supposedly based on his teachings often got lost in the details. In any case, neither the first, the thirteenth, nor any previous century can substitute for Christian teachers taking guidance from the past and articulating a Christian position on the great moral issues of our day. The *Catechism of the Catholic Church* says, "such indispensable adaptations are the responsibility of particular catechisms and, even more, of those who instruct the faithful."

Classroom Dialogue on Religion

Didache, as a follow up to *kerygma*, can be imagined as a simple extension of a single process. The doctrinal and moral implications of the gospel can be drawn out by a skilled interpreter. The place for such teaching is within the liturgy or overflowing from the liturgy. In the early church, the catechumen was given the fundamentals of creed, commandments, and sacraments before baptism, and then provided with a more complete picture of Christian teaching after initiation into the church. The Rite of Christian Initiation in today's church has been a fine adaptation of this early church practice.

For lifelong members of the church, the need for such instruction may not be so evident. But it has always been true, though more obvious today, that there are no automatic, lifelong Christians, no born Catholics. Horace Bushnell, in fighting against the image of one giant conversion in life, thought it possible that from infancy "the child is to grow up a Christian and never know himself as being otherwise." The same Bushnell is famous for the advocacy of "Christian nurture." To be an intelligent, practicing Christian in today's world supposes both a nurture generated by a community and intellectual conviction stimulated by knowledgeable and skilled teachers.

Understanding the Christian Message

The early church took on the world of classical learning. The Greek Fathers of the Church offered a "pedagogy in Christ" as an alternative worldview amid the Platonic, Stoic, Epicurean systems of the day. Later day Christians may think that such encounters cheapen the pure Christian gold, that an Origen became more a speculative philosopher than a Christian believer. Any correction, however, cannot divest Christian teaching of all cultural and philosophical relations.

Medieval thinkers developed a systematic dialogue between Christian belief and classical learning, as they knew it. The scholastic method called *sic at non* (yes and no) attempted to see both sides of an issue and resolve inconsistencies in commentaries on the Bible. The greatest exponent of the method, Thomas Aquinas, was considered dangerous because of his use of Aristotle, whom he refers to as "the philosopher" and who was available to Christian thinkers thanks to Arab Muslims. The word "theology" comes from Aristotle, not the Bible. But the assumption that Aquinas created a theological system to explain God is belied by the opening article of the *Summa* where Aquinas says: "Since we cannot know what God is but only what God is not, let us proceed to investigate the ways in which God does not exist."

Although Martin Luther was vitriolic in his condemnation of Aristotle, Luther's own understanding of faith and revelation is remarkably similar to that of Aquinas. Luther distrusted rational and mystical flights that went far beyond the sources, but Thomas Aquinas' work was grounded in his New Testament commentaries and his reading of the church fathers, especially Augustine. However, by Luther's day scholastic theology had hardened into a deadening system and was ready for a major overhaul. Erasmus, who battled with Luther over the limits of orthodoxy, was just as critical as Luther of the era's theology.

John Calvin reinstated a more systematic theology. Luther was a preacher; Calvin was a lawyer. Calvin insisted on the teaching role of the pastor and the importance of a continuing education, an emphasis that to this day is apparent in Presbyterian churches. The church, said Calvin, is "a *schola* from which our weakness does not allow us to be dismissed until we have been pupils for the whole course of our lives." School was a favorite metaphor of the Puritans, used to refer to the church and the family. Like all metaphors, the church as a school captures some aspects of church life but could be misleading in other respects.

In modern times, church and school were directly opposed. It was commonly said in the late nineteenth century, that education (school) was a replacement of the church. These days that claim is not made with the same confidence. The Christian religion and other religions have shown not only tenacity but also resurgence. The assumption still holds in many institutions of higher learning that religion and education are incompatible. That attitude cannot simply be dismissed by church leaders; it is the world of the present and future generations of Christians.

The only way for the church to counter this assumption is to sponsor serious schools of its own. Such schools can run the gamut from a kindergarten in the parish basement to a university with outstanding academic credentials. The church obviously needs ministerial schools which assume a Christian commitment and which concentrate on developing professional skills. A dramatic change has occurred in the Catholic seminary; whereas it was once strictly for clergy preparation, it is now also populated by women and men who are not preparing for priestly ordination but for other ministries. Even with a seminary population or with students in graduate programs of pastoral ministry, there has to be respect for an inquiring and sometimes doubting mind. Contemporary challenges to Christian doctrines and morals need to be candidly faced.

Dialogue has to characterize a classroom or else we are not serious in bringing people into a room designed for verbal exchange. I always say to students at the beginning of a course: "Dialogue is endless; we cannot do that but there should be more than a single exchange." The pattern is not "you ask questions, I give answers." Instead, "you ask a question, I respond, then I ask if you wish to respond further." On any complicated issue there is no final answer, but dialogue may bring us closer to the truth. I ask students to put their words on the table between us. I presume no license to enter into their minds, but their presence in the classroom signals a willingness to discuss the words that are between us.

I have said previously that neither storytelling, preaching, nor lecturing is the language of the classroom. These languages are presupposed by academic instruction and they supply much of the content for the questioning and criticizing in the classroom. Of course, every academic instructor does occasionally bring in stories, sermons, and lectures, either because of the deficiencies in the students' backgrounds or as a relief from the intense work of academic criticism. Students don't mind an occasional story; they can even bear with a little preaching. But by the third grade a student knows that the teacher should not always be preaching.

Lecturing, reading from a text or notes, can also provide a change of pace. At the college level, it is a temptation for both professors and students to confuse teaching with lecturing and the copying of notes. College students should do the reading before class and come prepared to question what they have read. The professor's job is not to supply information but to ask about the meaning, the ambiguities, and the alternate possibilities of such information.

This questioning of what the student already knows may seem possible as a method only at the university level. Admittedly, a six year old has less content to work with than the eighteen year old (or thirty-eight or sixty-eight year old). Our school system is upside down: it would make more sense if first graders went to school for fifteen minutes a day and graduate students spent four or five hours a day in class. Instead, part of the job of the elementary school becomes custodial, engaging in play and background work that one hopes is helpful to study and to learning in a classroom.

Putting people in classrooms for long periods of time before they are ready is a sure recipe for boredom and for the belief that classrooms are not part of the "real world." An element of critical thinking should be present from the beginning of school. Young children can be excited by the possibilities of language. They can also ask profound questions. Paul Tillich told of walking through a meadow with his six-year-old daughter and she suddenly asked: "Why is all this so? Here is the meadow, there the trees and there the mountain? Why isn't it all different?" Whether a satisfying answer can be supplied to a child, its propensity to ask questions and to raise doubts should not be killed off before they have had time to fully emerge.

Understanding Religion

Teaching religiously today also includes the study of religions and religious insights other than those in our own tradition, oftentimes those which conflict with it, challenge it, or call it to account.
—Fashion Me a People, p. 116

I have argued for many years that every person needs a twofold religious education: formation in the practices of their own religion and an understanding of religion. The church's educational ministry is mostly, though not entirely, about the first: learning to be a Christian by living in a Christian community, participating in the liturgy, following the moral guidance of Christian tradition.

Some of the second aspect—understanding religion—can be carried out in catechetical and theological instruction. Competent teachers in a Sunday School, a Catholic high school, or an adult inquiry class strive for understanding. The dialogue relates different strands of the tradition. A Scripture scholar or a church historian is always working to understand how one interpretation is related to another. The dialogue intrinsic to understanding religion can therefore be exemplified in the dialogue within a tradition. The task of understanding religion(s) includes understanding one's own religion.

At the time of the New Testament writing, the *didache* or instruction might not have been assumed to go further than understanding the doctrines and practices of the Christian life. The Christian today is faced with a different situation, starting with the very meaning of religion. The Christian Church absorbed the word religion from the Romans to describe proper practice. Religion was a virtue not an institution. Thomas Aquinas treats religion as one aspect of the virtue of justice. Even Calvin's title *Institutes of the Christian Religion* could be translated as Instructions in Christian Practice.

The meaning of religion that we assume today, religion as a social institution, is of late sixteenth-century origin. One might say that the first two religions were called Catholic and Protestant. Rather quick-

Not much serious dialogue between religions took place before the twentieth century. We are probably only at the threshold of the interreligious dialogue that is to come. Each religion has its own language and the outsider has to work diligently to understand the peculiar sayings and outrageous-sounding claims of a religious group. One cannot simply extract sentences out of a body of doctrine and presume to understand it. The task is so intimidating that one may wish to avoid it but that avenue is closing.

The good news is that almost everyone is as ignorant as I am. The bad news is that almost everyone is as ignorant as I am. Wherever I am in the knowledge of religions, I can begin to understand the religion of those people I encounter. H.G. Wells said that we are in a race between education and disaster. Events of the last century would not likely lead him to change his mind.

ly, those two were folded into diverse parts of one religion called Christianity. But now the word was available to historians, and later to social scientists and anthropologists, for naming Jewish, Muslim, Buddhist, or Hindu as religions.

Many of the people who are assigned this designation resent and reject it. Jews often object that they don't have a religion though Christians do. Evangelical Christians sometimes contrast Christian faith and world religions; other people have religion, we have faith. Karl Barth famously summed up this attitude with the statement that "religion is unbelief." The brunt of Barth's attack was not Buddhism or Islam but "Christian religion," the reifying of faith into an external system. Dietrich Bonhoeffer's call for a "religionless Christianity" was not an entirely new idea. Devout believers in God do not think of themselves as "having a religion."

The term "religion" does emphasize the external, what is evident to a scholar who wants to study a people's beliefs and practices. For many Christians, that is the drawback in referring to the Christian religion. However, the advantage in the term religion is that it makes comparison and dialogue possible. Just as the use of "religion" to include Catholics and Protestants was the first step on the way to toleration and then to mutual understanding, so also interreligious dialogue is indispensable today for world tolerance and understanding.

Before modern times, religion existed only in the singular; there was only one true religion. Religion as the term is used today always implies a plurality even when used in the singular. To say that understanding religion is an essential part of everyone's education means that we need to understand our own religion in relation to other religions. Logically, the term religious education would be unnecessary if its practice did not include more than one religion.

Some Christians, as I have indicated, are dead set against any religious dialogue. They simply deny that Christianity is one religion among many. But dialogue, intelligently and responsibly practiced, does not mean giving up one's own identity and beliefs. You can appreciate another person's beliefs only if you have convictions of your own. Early in life one has to acquire beliefs before any widespread comparison is possible. Immersing a young child into a discussion of multiple religions would likely lead to confusion not understanding. I have seen fifth-grade curricula that cover Hindu, Buddhist, Jewish, Muslim, and Christian religions. Even if fifth-graders were ready for all that, I can't imagine there are many teachers prepared to teach such a curriculum. A better first step would be to have intelligent discussion of religion as it surfaces in the study of the country's history and in the study of literature.

Learning religion is similar to learning language. You start with whatever you speak and move out to another language, usually one that is similar to your own. You don't become a linguist by studying one other language, but the experience of studying another language helps to make intelligible one's own. While the teacher of English grammar has struggled to get you to see the point of the subjunctive or of non-restrictive clauses, you get the point when studying German or French. If you try learning Chinese or Japanese, you are forced to think harder about the structure of language, English included.

A teacher of Islamic studies told me that his classes are filled with Jewish students—who are trying to understand Judaism. Islam is different from but structurally similar to Jewish religion. With some of the students' desired suspension of emotional involvement, it is perfectly logical to learn Judaism by taking a course in Islam. In my experience of Jewish-Christian conversation, the usual result of the dialogue is that the Jews become more Jewish and the Christians become more Christian, only more intelligently so. That happens when each party speaks from its own perspective but with a respect for the view of the other party. Jews and Christians are dialogue partners, even if at times the relation has been one of violence, insults, or silence.

CHAPTER SEVEN

Compassion and Service

In the New Testament, the word for service, diakonia, *which has also come to be translated as "ministry" is used in two ways. Sometimes the word has a general sense, referring to the entire range of the serving and ministering activities of the community. On other occasions it is particular and specific, designating such activities as serving at table, providing hospitality to guests, supplying the necessities of life or acting on behalf of the poor.* —Fashion Me a People, p. 144

Maria Harris's opening statement to her chapter on service captures several of the paradoxes that surround this fifth and final form of educational ministry. The peculiar character of this ministry can be seen by comparing it to community, the first ministry. Just as it might seem that community is simply the prerequisite of educational activities, so service might seem to be a result of such activities. However, a fuller understanding of community and the nature of teaching-learning, leads to the conclusion that community can be understood as inclusive of all ministry. The church's ministry begins and ends with community; all of its activities would fall short if they were not expressive of community. The peculiar way that community teaches is by being there.

As Maria points out, something parallel can be said of service. A full understanding of service and an understanding of how education occurs, reveal service to be a name for all ministries. Without a sense of service running throughout all its activities, the church's claim to be the people of God would ring hollow. The doing of service is not what we are educated for; rather service is itself a powerful teacher. But just as community is not as easy to grasp as its casual current use implies, so service is always in danger of being horribly misunderstood and used exploitatively.

What is at stake in this discussion of service is the nature of power and how Christians are called to act in a world that constantly misunderstands and misuses power. Power is sometimes understood as a very desirable good; the church, like other organizations, can become power hungry. In reaction, some people see power as an evil that is only to be restrained or condemned. The church and its individual members often feel powerless up against destructive uses of power that seem to be everywhere. Lest the church exhaust itself by expending its resources in all directions, it has to be clear about the source and the nature of its own power.

In line with a theme running throughout this book, service can be viewed as both a local and a global issue. For the church to be credible in this area, service needs expression in the help that is offered to one or a few struggling creatures. But for such help to be effective beyond the moment and also spread to many others who are in need of help, the church has to give witness with global organizations. It has to speak truth to those principalities that are interested only in serving themselves.

Both locally and globally the church has to draw upon its own power, exemplified in the teachings and the life of Jesus. At the local level, I will concentrate on the church's response to the suffering brought on by grinding poverty. At the global level, I will concentrate on the church's vocation at this time in history to be a witness for peace and nonviolence.

The two themes have obvious connections. Poverty is a continual violence in the lives of the poor. The crimes that poor people commit are evident but the crimes of government and business policies against the poor are usually hidden. Wars employ the poor (consider the voluntary army of the United States or the 300,000 child soldiers in the world), and the devastations of war fall hardest upon the poor. Maria's chapter has dozens of wonderful examples of church organizations and practices. I will limit my discussion to the nature of service and these two themes of poverty and peace.

Serve, Service, Servant

> *Because of its close association with the term servant, service is also approached with hesitation: ours is not a society of servants, and servant classes have almost entirely disappeared. Most people want neither to have servants nor to be servants.* —Fashion Me a People, p. 145

The English words "serve" and "service" have an undistinguished history. They are closely allied to the term "slavery," the ultimate degradation of the human being. A servant is a step up from being a slave but it is still not a desirable condition for a human being. While serving rich and obnoxious people still dominates the lives of many poor people, at least we no longer think that being a servant or a slave is a good and necessary condition for some people. Aristotle thought that some people were born to be slaves. On this point we seem to have made progress, at least in our theories.

The paradoxical idea of becoming a slave or a servant *voluntarily* has not died out. It has played a central role in the history of Christianity. The Bible uses the words "serve," "serving," and especially "servant" more than 1300 times. Choosing to be a servant is praised. There is a whole body of secular literature on "servant leadership," which came out of the business world but found wide acceptance among church leaders. Christians who use the language of servanthood are trying to follow in the footsteps of Jesus who became a servant to all. One can say that service is truly the primary word that the earliest followers of Jesus used to describe the relational quality of Jesus' actions and his words. Jesus came to serve.

In trying to adopt the position of a servant, a person might be accused of posturing. A well-educated, rich, white person who moves into a ghetto is not trapped in the same way as a child who is born into poverty from birth. And does anyone really believe that the CEO of a corporation is a servant of the people? On the other hand, if a person does succeed in identifying with suffering and poverty, the danger is in seeming to glorify suffering as a good in itself.

This attitude of seeming to praise suffering is an accusation especially leveled at Christianity (to a lesser extent at Judaism). Christianity holds up the "suffering servant" as its witness to the world. In the early church, the cross showed the risen Lord in all his glory. But from the twelfth century onward, the crucifix took over and the focus was on the excruciating sufferings of the Savior.

The reaction to the film *The Passion of the Christ* was a startling reminder that there is still an enormous gap in understanding suffering in the work of Jesus and its place in Christian life. The film was an unrelieved portrayal of suffering, presumably designed to evoke pious sentiments. The film was ridiculed and attacked long before it was released on Ash Wednesday of 2004. To almost everyone's astonishment, it did six hundred million dollars worth of business. Perhaps the film did some good, but for many people it seemed to focus too narrowly on suffering.

Near the beginning of Albert Camus's novel *The Plague,* the preacher Paneloux gives a sermon in which he castigates the congregation and tells them that God has sent this plague as punishment for their sins and a test of their faith. The atheist physician, Rieux, comments: "Paneloux is a man of learning, a scholar. He hasn't come in contact with death; that's why he can speak with such assurance of the Truth—with a capital T. But every country priest who visits his parishioners and has heard a man gasping for breath on his deathbed thinks as I do. He'd try to relieve human suffering before trying to point out its excellence." Later in the novel, when Paneloux is himself hit by the illness, he becomes more compassionate. He now shares the suffering and is less inclined to praise it.

Nietzsche's assault on Christianity was on a religion of pity that glorifies weakness. I first encountered Nietzsche's ideas in 1958 while reading Victor Frankl's *Man's Search for Meaning.* Frankl several times cites Nietzsche as saying that "he who has a why to life can bear almost any how." I thought that was a strong apology for Christianity and I did not realize until reading Nietzsche that it is his point of attack. Nietzsche accuses Christianity of glorifying suffering by giving it a meaning. The priest class encourages weakness and suffering; the poor are kept in place by the promises of a reward hereafter for sufferings patiently borne.

Pity versus Compassion

Nietzsche was not without evidence that Christianity has at times been at the service of the rich by keeping the poor in place by praising weakness and suffering. But the Christianity he assumes is a distorted version filtered through Rousseau. The ethics that Rousseau expounds is centered on pity, which Rousseau thought was the one moral sentiment we are born with. Pity is an isolated feeling that an individual has for a helpless creature; it's a pity when someone suffers and we feel sorry for him or her. In contrast to pity, compassion means to suffer with someone; it is not a looking down but a movement toward. Compassion generates action in a community to relieve suffering. Rousseau was quite successful in situating pity at the center of ethics, especially in the United States. Other countries fear that United States foreign policy is often beholden to the whims of pity; waves of sentiment initiate and then reverse policies. Any story that evokes a sentiment of pity (a trapped animal, for example) plays well on television. But compassionate efforts to relieve poverty, provide health care, and improve schools have a more difficult case to make. The compassionate religious person does not understand why there is such suffering in the world, will sometimes scream in protest at God, but will not let those feelings interfere with the effort to relieve suffering.

One hopeful sign in the writing of ethics during the last twenty years has been a new attention given to the ideas of care and compassion. This emphasis has come from women writers new to the field. How far compassion will penetrate to the main story of ethics is not yet clear. From the beginning of this emerging attention to compassion, many men have been inclined to relegate compassion to a feminist concern. Compassion is good for women and perhaps even for men in their private lives. But justice is what the bigger world needs, not compassion. A dichotomy of justice and compassion threatens to undermine the renewal that compassion can bring to ethics.

Compassion is a re-visioning of strength and weakness. It recognizes that suffering is the human condition from which we start. But there is suffering that touches the profound greatness of humanity and there is suffering that is useless, painful, and destructive of humanity. Not surprisingly, humans get confused about suffering, which they try to flee from and succeed only in entangling themselves in worse suffering. Rousseau was more accurate in what he thought was the other innate sentiment: a fear of death. To be a suffering animal is to be reminded that we die. As a result we try to segregate suffering to moments of illness and we convince ourselves that such moments are a passing phase. Simone Weil wrote: "Every creature that is threatened by death secretes falsehood as a way of avoiding death. There is no love of the truth without a love of the cross." Death comes to almost everyone as a surprise: Who me? There must be some mistake. Elisabeth Kubler-Ross documented this "first stage of dying" as the denial of dying.

The Christian message is the audacious claim that suffering and death are redemptive, that suffering and death can be welcomed. It is hardly surprising that Christianity is thought to be morbid and masochistic by many more people than Nietzsche. It does have its share of morbid and masochistic people, but it is centered on life that puts death in proper perspective. The Christian view of power glorifies not the pain that sometimes accompanies suffering but the receptivity to suffering that is the basis of shared power, intimate love, and joy—despite pain.

The paradox of power lies in the fact that what initially appears to be weakness is where *human* strength lies. When it comes to *brute* strength, the human power is nowhere near the top. Even within the nonanimal world, the humans do not rank high in size, height, weight, and the power to dominate. A visitor from another planet would immediately conclude that a human being, who can get knocked over by a strong wind and who has to live in a world where the rule is to eat or be eaten, does not have a future. The strange thing is that only the humans know about the future at all, at least a long-term future. They take the world into themselves and imagine other possibilities than what has been given to them. Other animals instinctively associate with their own kind and struggle to dominate others. Human life begins by resembling nonhuman animals but humans quickly discover that they have another power in the capacity to choose. They can attend to some things and disregard other things. They can decide whether or not to allow a particular being into a relation of intimacy.

The human power is in receptivity and openness to others that leads to the sharing of a richer life. The word power means potential, possible, passive. Passivity may suggest being submissive and subservient. But the human possibility—its receptive passivity—is its greatest power. Medieval philosophy distinguished between active intelligence and passive intelligence. Active intelligence goes outward to gather data, but passive intelligence is intelligence proper, the power to become other without ceasing to be oneself. This meaning of power is the context of Paul's paradoxical statement that "power is made perfect in weakness...whenever I am weak, then I am strong" (2 Corinthians 12:9,10).

With others of its own kind a human can listen, respond, and work cooperatively or else the human can try to protect its space and fragile existence by fending off competition. Since humans feel threatened from the moment of birth or even earlier, their constant temptation is to trust in brute strength. But since they aren't really brutes, their attempts to act like a brute produce far more destruction than activities of other animals. To say that a human is acting like a brute is insulting to the other animals. Human mistakes about the nature of their power can be more accurately likened to a hurricane, plane crash, or a burst of dynamite.

Humans never escape from the fears at life's beginning and their precarious position throughout life. Sometimes they have to resort to the dominative kind of power, exercising one-way control rather than engaging in cooperative activity. Such a one-way use of power against a resistant world is force. Force is a fact of life, something that humans use against the environment and occasionally against other humans. Force is always suspect and needs justification and restraint by human power. Even against the physical environment, humans are slowly coming to recognize that they cannot just shove it around any way they please; the rivers and oceans will not only shove back but also overrun human settlements.

In human dealings, force is often a violation of the other's free will. However, force can be a good, as it is in restraining a child from running into traffic, or force is sometimes a sad necessity, as in a policeman stopping a would-be rapist. While a limited use of force is a form of power that can be nonviolent, no human has a right to use unrestrained force. Violence is not an extension of human power but its opposite.

Because Christianity is based on a paradox of power, it is subject to terrible and tragic misinterpretation by people who may collapse the paradox prematurely. A young person might not be ready to grasp the full extent of the paradox. That is the reason why a person's Christian education should not stop in childhood. Christianity is a lifelong journey; its central teaching, as John Calvin said, requires lifelong learning.

I once gave a talk in Dublin on the theme that the Beatitudes are not well understood until middle age. I said that one can only appreciate giving up your life after you have acquired a life. Church leaders telling children and adolescents that they should lay down their life is dangerous. I can still picture the angry response of one young woman who said I did not appreciate that young people can be good Christians too. I tried to explain that I was not excluding young people. I was opposing the idea that conversion is something that happens at age nine, twelve, or eighteen. Christian conversion is a cyclical movement that culminates in middle age and old age. (The horrifying extension of preaching self-sacrifice to adolescents is seen in parts of the world where older men encourage teenagers to be suicide bombers in the name of their religion. If middle-aged men want to kill themselves, that's one thing; but attaching bombs to the bodies of boys and girls is despicable.)

Serving the Neighbor

Social care takes shape in familiar ways: feeding the hungry, giving drink to the thirsty, sheltering the homeless, clothing the naked, ministering to those who are ill, sick or dying. At its best, and when this is possible, it is toward helping others to help themselves.
—Fashion Me a People, p. 149

Vatican II's document *The Church in the Modern World* begins with the assertion that "Christians share the joy and hope, the griefs and anguish of [the people] of our time, especially of those who are poor or afflicted." Note that the sharing is of joy and hope as well as of grief and anguish. The poor and the afflicted are not helped by pity from on high. They can be helped by compassionate efforts to find joy and hope in the midst of problems that cannot be cured and by compassionate efforts on the side of the poor and afflicted where relief is possible. As the U.S. Catholic bishops said in *Our Hearts Were Burning Within Us*, "An active faith bears the fruit of justice and compassion through active outreach to those in need." Compassionate action for justice is simply the other side of prayer, the sign that we have understood what the words of our prayers mean. Liturgy is a centripetal movement in a language of intimacy to celebrate the life of the community. Service to the poor is a centrifugal movement in any language that works to help those most in need.

This exercise of power has to be shown in local concerns of cooperation that genuinely help those in need. There are many kinds of deprivation and a person's feelings of wants are relative to the situation. The church or even the United States government cannot guarantee prosperity and health to every U.S. citizen, let alone the whole world. Nonetheless, respect for human dignity demands that we provide what Henry Shue calls basic rights, especially the rights to subsistence and physical security. The first amendment rights of speech, assembly, press, and religion are rightly cherished in the United States, but such rights cannot be exercised if people are starving or are in constant fear for their life. The church has a twofold role of service here: to provide what help it can offer in interpersonal ways and to be a voice on behalf of the poor.

Until the university changed its class scheduling, I was able to work for fifteen years in the soup kitchen that the church runs on Mondays. A real effort was made to provide a good meal in a humane atmosphere. But every Monday as I washed dishes I would wonder if we were only encouraging the irresponsibility of city and federal governments. Why are there thousands of homeless and hungry people in this very rich neighborhood? It is unrealistic to expect churches, synagogues, and the like to handle this problem. Feeding a few hundred people is not a sufficient response to widespread poverty and homelessness. But when people are starving, you feed them if you can; protest against the government is for another day.

The food that is shared should not have any hooks in it; food is not a tool to increase church membership. A church that reaches outward will probably attract new members but practicing compassion is not a means to something else. An individual Christian can provide help to the poor; an organized church can do more. James Forbes, pastor at Riverside church and one of the great churchmen in New York, says, "Nobody gets to heaven without a reference letter from the poor."

It is quite remarkable that the one clear criterion that the New Testament offers for the final judgment is whether you practiced the corporal works of mercy. Maria lists them in the above passage: feed the hungry, give drink to the thirsty, shelter the homeless, and visit the imprisoned. The logic of divine judgment is: "Just as you did it to one of the least of these who are members of my family, you did it to me" (Matthew 25:40). Meister Eckhart reminds us, "It is better to feed the hungry than to see even such visions as St. Paul saw."

The call is not to throw food or money in the direction of the poor. The beautiful words "charity" and "welfare" have acquired negative connotations from their misuse in situations of pity or in the workings of heartless bureaucracy. Charity ought to be the kind of help that respects the poor person and gives hope that something better is possible. A person confined to his or her apartment may need food, but he or she may also need conversation to accompany the meal. Where I washed dishes, the law students would work with homeless people to get them city services that they were entitled to, a bigger help than giving them a meal.

For Christian charity to be true service, the poor cannot be an object of pity. Compassionate action is a listening, an answering, and then a moving in the direction of mutuality. The one who is teaching or serving has something to give but is aware that positions could easily be reversed. The Epistle to the Hebrews says, "Remember those who are in prison, as though you are in prison with them; those who are being tortured, as though you yourself were being tortured" (13:3). Identifying with the imprisoned and tortured, the sick and aged, the poor and humiliated, should not take a great feat of imagination. One sharp pain in the chest, one dip in the wrong part of the economy, one mix-up in the judicial system, and even the "self-made" person discovers that life has always been dependent on strangers.

Compassionate action on behalf of the poor is difficult to design. Even with the best intentions of those who are trying to help, the poor are likely to feel like objects of pity. The words "serve" and "service" cannot entirely hide the imbalance of power. Vincent de Paul told his disciples to comport themselves so that "the poor will forgive you the bread you give them." In a culture that glorifies independence, it is humiliating to be on the receiving end of a handout. To receive can be the greatest human power; but to receive can be a sign of complete impotence. Mary Douglas writes, "Though we laud charity as a Christian virtue we know that it wounds."

The way in which the poor and the suffering keep their dignity is by giving back whatever they can. I said that the bread should not have a hook in it; the donor should make it a gift and not expect payment of any kind. But that attitude does not exclude the recipient's giving in return. The poor keep their self-respect by giving. In the soup kitchen, some of the guests who were served a meal would join in washing the dishes. Their action was neither requested nor expected. But it would change the tone of the whole operation from being charity for the helpless to a cooperative work of helping those who are at present in need.

Acting on someone's behalf can have two nearly opposite meanings. The term "behalf" started out as a reference to oneself and which half of oneself is given preference. In time the word became used for taking the half or the side of a group. To speak on behalf of a group can mean joining with them in their efforts. But it can also mean being a substitute for them, speaking instead of letting them speak. If a group cannot raise its voice at all, for example, disabled children or permanently comatose patients in our hospitals, someone may have to speak for them. But the poor and the unschooled, who have not had much opportunity to speak on their own behalf, can use help not by people who substitute for them but by people who on their behalf help them to speak for themselves. As Gustavo Gutierrez has written, "We will have an authentic theology of liberation only when the oppressed themselves can freely raise their voice and express themselves directly and creatively in society and in the heart of the People of God."

Because human power is based on receptivity, those who are looked down on as weak and helpless may be the real power centers holding the world together. In saying that, there is a danger that Christianity can romanticize poverty and suffering. The poor may be always with us, and the poor may usually be more virtuous than the rich, but poverty is cruel and debilitating. At a national level, we do not need a "war on poverty," a bad metaphor that goes back at least to 1913. We simply need fairer laws than those that leave some people obscenely rich and millions of children lacking minimum care.

When Bill Clinton became president he promised to end welfare as we know it. In 1996, his promise was carried out but not in a way he had foreseen. One has to be suspicious of a bill named "The Personal Responsibility and Work Opportunity Reconciliation Act." Two years previously, the Republican congress had succeeded in equating the phrase "personal responsibility" with "cutting government welfare." The consequence of that change of language was predictable. In signing the bill, Clinton admitted that there were some disgraceful provisions in it that he hoped could be corrected later. It eliminated 300,000 disabled children from aid, presumably so that they could go out to work. Some people were apparently helped to get off the government's welfare roll. Having salaried work outside the home instead of depending on government grants can be a big boost to one's self-respect. But that could only happen with support at the state and local levels. Subsequent changes in policy have removed some of the worst provisions but compassionate action to support human dignity and relieve poverty has not triumphed.

When the welfare bill was being discussed in 1996, Senator Daniel Patrick Moynihan said he was surprised that there was so little protest. In fact, he said the only group that raised consistent protest at his door was the United States Conference of Catholic Bishops. The Catholic Church at the national level has a fairly good record of protest in the name of the poor. Of course, when the National Catholic Welfare Conference was started in the early twentieth century, the Catholics were the poor, or at least a large slice of the poor. Now those earlier Catholic immigrant groups—Irish, Italian, East European—are among the wealthier part of the population. The economically poor population still counts many Catholics and Protestants who are in need of the church's voice. And the mission of the churches is not only concern for other Christians but for other citizens of the United States and the world beyond.

Serving World Peace

Witness the U.S. bishops' statements on the economy and peace, the continuing testimony of church people before congressional committees, and the lobbying efforts of concerned religious groups.
—Fashion Me a People, p. 153

Questions about the use of power at the international level are obviously more complex than at the interpersonal level. Nevertheless, personal attitudes carry over and international decisions are the work of men and women who have their own slant on power, force, violence, and war. While a misunderstanding in interpersonal situations can be distressing for the individuals involved, a misunderstanding and misuse of power internationally can be disastrous for the whole world. Unfortunately, the reduction of power to force, and the resulting equation of force and war, is the standard use of language in international affairs. The world will never find peace if it is assumed that there are only two choices: war as synonymous with force, or pacifism as equivalent to an absence of force.

For contributing to an alternative, the church has to serve in two ways. It has to be a witness to a just peace by communities that are peace loving. A local church does not have to say much in the way of preaching peace to others, just stay on its message directed to its own members. The second way that the church has to serve peace is exemplified by Pope John XXIII's encyclical *Pacem in Terris*. That document was addressed to the whole world and has been followed by several church pronouncements that have engaged a secular reaction. These works are inspired by the teaching of Jesus and the witness of Christian saints, but they speak the language of today's ethics, politics, and international relations. They attempt to persuade men and women of good will that there is another way to address the questions of war and peace.

The church through its leaders has to speak with some humility on this issue because its own record is far from spotless. After an early period when the followers of Jesus refused to serve in the military and opposed all war, the church became entangled in imperial politics and the wars that have bedeviled European history. Still, throughout Christian history there have been voices opposed to war and movements to limit war. The rules that have restrained modern war (Geneva Accords) are a continuation of medieval writing on legitimate reasons needed for going to war and ethical restraints in the midst of war. Establishing rules for a so-called just war was the best that world leaders could devise in the past but it is inadequate for the twenty-first century.

Many people look back nostalgically on the Second World War as a "good war" instead of a tragedy of fifty million deaths brought on by the incompetence and indecisiveness of world leaders in the 1920s and '30s. The magnitude of the next full-scale war may dwarf that of World War II. Of course, it would be utterly irrational for any nation to unleash such fury and it may seem therefore that it will never happen. But if one reads the inside accounts of the Cuban missile crisis in 1962, it is evident that the world was minutes away from nuclear holocaust. Both President John F. Kennedy and Nikita Khrushchev had to resist the advice of their closest advisors that they could not show weakness by backing down. It was, as Arthur Schlesinger has said, the most dangerous moment in the history of the world. How was catastrophe avoided? Robert McNamara, one of the key players, says: dumb luck.

In the Cuban missile crisis, Kennedy and Khrushchev created a diplomatic dance of agreement that could only be partially revealed to their respective publics. They did manage to cooperate in the use of power, the alternative to violence. That is what diplomacy is for, but it has become more difficult for diplomats to do their job. Instead of the force of argument to find positions mutually acceptable, loud threats and bombs quickly become the currency. Any words from church leaders may seem hopelessly overmatched, but the choice between words and bombs is precisely the issue.

United States foreign policy has usually drawn on a primitive meaning of power. More specifically, power is equated with one form of power, namely, force. Joseph Nye recently coined a distinction between "hard power" and "soft power," which quickly became absorbed into international discussions. Unfortunately, Nye's two kinds of power are only two kinds of force. If we can't control people with a soft approach, such as cultural influence, then we can always hit them hard with bombs. Power that is the opposite of control, that is an invitation to cooperation, is not to be found in Nye's distinction.

Standing in the background is Max Weber and his writing at the beginning of the twentieth century. Weber defined power as "the probability that one actor within a social relationship will be in a position to carry out his own will despite resistance." It is a small jump from that meaning of power to Weber's description of the state as the institution that can legitimately use violence. When power collapses into force, then force inevitably leads to violence. In international discussions, the use of force is a euphemism for going to war. Force as a shorthand for military force may seem harmless, but it is an obstacle to thinking realistically about how to deal with conflict.

When the European Union made its last desperate plea to the United States not to go to war against Iraq, its statement said, "War is not inevitable; the use of force should be the last resort." It would have been more logical and more practical to say, "War is not inevitable even though the use of force is." By equating force and war, they eliminated a discussion of all the uses of force that might have been successful, such as trade embargos, international inspections, and no-fly zones.

One notable exception to equating force and war is found in the "long telegram" by George Kennan, who was ambassador to Moscow at the end of World War II. His essay, published anonymously, was one of the most important diplomatic documents of the twentieth century. He uses the term "force" about a dozen times, never as a synonym for war, sometimes in explicit contrast to war. "Soviet pressure against the free institutions of the Western world can be constrained by the adroit and vigorous application of counter force. That force should take the form of diplomacy and covert action not war." In the forty subsequent years, Kennan's sane diplomatic view helped to keep the Soviet Union-United States standoff from degenerating into true war. (He thought that the Vietnam War from the start was a disaster.)

Kennan always insisted that his views were not based on morality. Although there is a moral tone to his writings, he thought morality had to be based on religion. Nevertheless, he was inspired by Protestant-Christian thinking on the created world as good but affected by sin. Kennan once said that Reinhold Niebuhr is the father of us all, in reference to Niebuhr's key role in laying the foundation of foreign policy as a tragic clash of competing national powers. Niebuhr unfortunately contributed to the dichotomy between morality at the individual level where the Sermon on the Mount could be a guide and a morality (or lack of morality) that comes from acting in the "national interest." Later in life, during the Vietnam War, Niebuhr expressed regret for his sharp dichotomy of "moral man and immoral society." He said that perhaps he should have read more Catholic and Jewish literature.

Niebuhr was not the first to dismiss the relevance of the Sermon on the Mount for international affairs. Max Weber contrasted an ethic of responsibility and an ethic of individual intention, embodied in the Sermon on the Mount. In Weber's view, nonviolence is fine for the individual, but statesmen have to govern with responsibility. Helmut Schmidt, Chancellor of West Germany in 1981, said, "It would be an error to understand the Sermon on the Mount as guidelines for governmental action." And in a famous speech to students in 1968, Herbert Marcuse did not dismiss but instead attacked: "With the Sermon on the Mount one cannot revolt....Nothing is more abominable than the preaching of love: 'Do not hate your opponent'—this in a world in which hate is everywhere institutionalized."

Marcuse's speech is particularly ironic; he is right that hatred is everywhere institutionalized but that's the reason why not hating your opponent is so badly needed to break the cycle of hatred. At least Marcuse's statement is more honest than polite reference to Jesus' teaching but no serious attention to what it says. It is insulting to Christian teaching to say that it is admirable between individuals but just doesn't measure up in the serious world of business and politics. Marcuse is right that the question is not where to locate love of enemies but whether that idea is absurd. It is absurd if power is only the force to dominate. If power is also a sharing of life made possible by receptivity, then love has a chance, even if against the odds. In Kenneth Boulder's words: "Know this: though love is weak and hate is strong, yet hate is short and love is very long."

If the Christian teaching embodied in the Sermon on the Mount is to influence national policy, some translation and interpretation is needed. The Sermon on the Mount is not about being selfless or allowing oneself to be stepped on. It is about turning enemies into political allies by acts of kindness and nonviolence. "Do good to those who hate you." This strategy is one that requires strength and courage. The point of receptive passivity is "mutual dismantling of hostility by a vigorous reconciliation benefiting the hater as well as the hated." Martin Luther King, Jr. defined faith as "a non-symmetrical response to violence." How one may react is not entirely predictable but it will be nonviolent activity.

Force is sometimes demanded, a holy anger at injustice and cruelty. That use of force can slip over into violence. In a violent world, even the attempt to resist violence can involve a person in unintended violence. Realistically, one has to acknowledge that individuals are not innocent of violence and no nation is. But that is no excuse for simply adding to the violence.

The individual Christian may simply say, "I'm opposed to war and I will protest against it." That may be enough for an individual, but an organized church response that has a chance of influencing policy has to articulate a position on the use of power. The term "pacifism" carries too much ideological baggage to be a basis for international policies. William James noted in his essay "The Moral Equivalent of War" that "the weakness of so much merely negative criticism is evident—pacifism makes no converts from the military party." Today it is even less likely that any government official would call him or herself a pacifist.

Thomas Merton, one of the great voices for peace in the twentieth century, said he would not describe himself as a pacifist. In *Seeds of Destruction* he gave four reasons, including the fact that pacifism depended solely on the conscience of the individual. Pacifism has been a negation of war but not a way to work out peace in a violent world. Erasmus, five centuries earlier, had the same problem as Merton. He realized that there would always be clashes between nation-states so long as they exist. For peace to be possible, the world has to have international institutions to mediate conflicts. We are finally getting to such institutions with the United Nations, the International Criminal Court, and various war tribunals. Any existing structures are fragile, to say the least, and under constant attack from people who equate power with military force. Christian teaching today has to be in support of the cooperative power of nonviolent action.

Catholic teaching on peace and war had begun to shift with Pope Leo XIII's encyclical *Rerum Novarum* in 1891. The encyclical's central concern was for an international order in which peace would be based on justice rather than on military force. The Pope called for a reevaluation of defensive war in a technological world. Pope Benedict XV at the beginning of World War I outlined the causes of war and methods for attaining peace. The Pope zeroed in on lack of mutual love, disregard of authority, class warfare, and gross materialism. The really startling change in tone was signaled by Pope John XXIII in his 1963 encyclical *Pacem in Terris*. Addressed to the whole world, the Pope condemned the arms race and called for structural reform of international systems of law. There was emphasis on transcending the dichotomy of just-war theory and pacifism. Something notably not said was an endorsing of the right of self-defense for peoples or states.

As could have been predicted, *Pacem in Terris* met with little enthusiasm in the United States. The Pope was dismissed as an old man dreaming dreams. But the issue had been forcefully raised so that the Second Vatican Council could not avoid it. At the fourth session of the Council in 1965, the bishops said that contemporary conditions "compel us to undertake an evaluation of war with an entirely new attitude....This Holy Synod makes its own the condemnation of total war already pronounced by recent popes." The emphasis was on the word total, which at the least included nuclear war. But the Council held back from condemning all war; it said that so long as there is not a sufficiently powerful international authority, "governments cannot be denied the right to legitimate defense once every means of peaceful settlement has been exhausted."

Attitudes about war were dramatically changing among Roman Catholics. At the end of the 1980s, a study called *The American Catholic People* found that at the start of the Vietnam War, Catholics were more hawkish than the rest of the country. At the end of that war, Catholics were more dovish than other citizens—and remained that way. At the beginning of the 1980s, Catholic bishops were scrambling to keep up both with the international situation and their own people. The bishops engaged in a fine example of democratic process by publishing a first draft of a letter they were writing on peace. After three drafts, thirty-six witnesses, and extensive debate, the bishops issued *A Pastoral Letter on Peace*.

At one point in the deliberations, the White House tried to interfere, fearful of losing the support of staunch anti-communists. The bishops sent the ex-seminarian messenger back to the White House. President Ronald Reagan and other top officials correctly sensed that this change was not a flip in one direction that might easily be changed by a flop in the opposite direction. Old-time cardinals who had laboriously argued themselves to the limits of just war theory were not likely to change their minds tomorrow. The bishops declared in their letter: "Peacemaking is not an optional commitment. It is a requirement of our faith. We are called to be peacemakers, not by any movement of the moment, but by Our Lord Jesus."

No one knows how much this letter may have influenced the Reagan-Gorbachev negotiations of the late 1980s. The bishops made an eloquent appeal to the whole world to say no to nuclear weapons and other weapons of mass destruction, no to an arms race, which robs the poor and the vulnerable, and no to a choice between terror and surrender. It was one of the finest moments that the U.S. Catholic bishops have ever had, both for the thoughtful discussion and the final product. George Kennan, who one would expect to be a tough critic, wrote, "This paper...may fairly be described as the most profound and searching inquiry yet conducted by any responsible collective body into the relations of nuclear weaponry, and indeed of modern war in general, to moral philosophy, to politics, and to the conscience of the national state."

In 1988, the Catholic bishops followed up their letter on peace with *A Letter on Economic Justice for All*. As I noted at the beginning of this chapter, there is an intrinsic relation between war and poverty. A letter dealing with justice for the poor was therefore a fitting sequel to the bishops' success at getting attention with their letter on peace. The bishops asserted that "every economic decision and institution must be judged in light of whether it protects or undermines the dignity of the human person...what it does for and to people and...how it permits all to participate in it."

The bishops would seem to have had a receptive audience for this message. In a 2005 poll of Catholics eighteen years old or older, eighty-four percent said that what is most central to being a Catholic is helping the poor and belief in Jesus' resurrection. Some people found distressing the lack of attention to other doctrines but the choice of those two doctrines provides a good start for catechetical instruction. In the

New Testament, when Paul was accepted by Peter, John, and James, he says, "They asked only one thing, that we remember the poor, which was actually what I was eager to do" (Galatians 2:10).

For their letter on economic justice, the bishops attempted to use the same collegial process as they had for their letter on peace. It was no fault of theirs that this second letter did not get the same media attention. Poverty is never a topic in season, except for the poor.

I was hoping that the bishops would next take up the topic of the church in America: North, South, and Central. A start was perhaps made with the Synod of the Americas in 1997, but the plural use of America is a sign that the issue is not being faced. A clarifying of America as distinct from the United States is urgently needed, and I cannot imagine any institution except the Catholic Church that might effectively address this topic. A truly American synod is needed; bishops in the United States would have to learn Spanish to give some credibility to the proceedings.

The United States government certainly has no inclination to clarify the relation between the name of the country and an idea about the country. From the time of its coining in 1507, the term "America" had a double meaning: religious and geographical. As the name of Europe's dream of the promised land, America had a religious meaning. As a geographical term, America had a continental meaning. When the British American colonies became a separate nation, the new republic identified itself with the religious meaning by calling itself the United States of America. With that name, the United States also laid claim to continental America: North, South, and Central. Of the four words in the country's name, the key word was the third: *of.* If the country had been called the United States *in* America, the geographical meaning might have flourished and the religious meaning might have been held in check. The United States could have located itself in the northeast part of America, instead of thinking that it owns the American continent.

The religious idea of America is dangerous unless there is resistance to an idolatrous patriotism. Because "America" is biblical in origin, it is up to Jewish and Christian religions to be the main counter force that reminds the United States that it is not America. What has always been a danger with the country suddenly got much worse in 2001. The confusion between a nation-state and a religious idea had always been open to exploitation but until recently there had been some restraint.

The United States government is now more than ever tempted to think it has a divine mandate for its policies. The first name given to the military strike in Afghanistan was "operation infinite justice."

In the week that followed September 11, 2001, there seemed to be some real soul-searching in the country. But by the end of the week, the metaphor of war had taken over. A "war on terror" is illogical in that war is the worst form of terror. But the metaphor so used made it much easier to slide into a real war, a preemptive war against a perceived enemy. In 2001, I described the situation as analogous to a schoolyard filled with children. The schoolyard bully had just taken a sucker punch. The rest of the kids actually felt some sympathy for the big guy, along with some repressed glee. All eyes were on the bully. Would he lash out in violent retribution to whoever was near or would he decide that if even the big guy isn't safe, a new order is needed in the schoolyard.

The immediate response did seem restrained but subsequently the actions of the big guy lost him any sympathy. The cycle of violence continues. Power understood only as force, force understood as war, continue to rule. But hope has to be sustained with the only power that can challenge that rule. "Violence is a method by which the ruthless few can subdue the passive many. Nonviolence is a means by which the active many can overcome the ruthless few."

Epilogue

Maria Harris approached death as she had lived her life, with courage, candor, and a gentle sense of humor. Nearly all this story takes place either in Montauk, Long Island, or in New York City. In Montauk, a tiny fishing and retirement village at the tip of Long Island, Maria, with her usual outgoingness, had developed a group of women friends in the town. They were anxious to do anything they could to help during Maria's illness. However, for medical reasons it was preferable to spend most of the time in New York's Greenwich Village where we lived in an apartment owned by New York University.

People outside of New York can find it difficult to believe me when I say that during this time we were overwhelmed with kindness and compassion. From physicians and social workers to cab drivers and subway riders, people were unfailingly kind and helpful. Some of that reaction was undoubtedly due to Maria's personality, which seemed to bring out the best in people. Illness dimmed that light, but only death extinguished the sparkle of her personality.

Ominous Signs
(Summer 2000 to Summer 2001)

If dementia is in fact genetic in origin, then no doubt there are telltale signs before its onset. Usually the signs are not obvious except in retrospect. I think Maria began to have problems in the middle of the year 2000 but at the time I thought any problem was minor and passing. Maria had been amazingly free of health problems. The first noticeable problem came on a trip to Israel in July 2000. We were going to a meeting of an organization called ISREV (International Seminar on Religious Education and Values). Both of us had been members since 1980. Maria was always a bright light, livening up both the academic and social aspects of the meeting. Maria leading the group in singing on the last night of the conference was always a high point.

The trip started badly; British Airways had problems that delayed the flight four hours. We knew as we took off from Newark that we had missed the connecting flight to Tel Aviv. We finally did get there, embarrassed to be twenty-four hours late. Maria seemed tired understandably enough, but it turned out she had an infection requiring medical attention. At the time, it just seemed a bother; she had developed a similar problem on the fifteen-hour flight from Seoul a few years earlier. Maria was fascinated by the medical care she was given by a Palestinian physician. Still, she was subdued for the whole conference. It proved to be the last conference she was able to attend.

She had some uneasy moments at presentations that fall, but I still thought it was overwork and that she only needed rest. But she had an experience in Erie, Pennsylvania, in the late fall that shocked her. She was doing a weekend workshop, and on the Saturday afternoon her mind went completely blank. She was terribly embarrassed at having to cancel the remainder of the program, even though her hosts were only concerned for her health. This incident was indeed worrisome but I could still hope that the problem was a passing blip. But for her that was the end of what she had been doing so well for twenty-five years. She feared having a repeat of the forgetting.

I tried to coax her into taking on a non-threatening situation. I said that the women at Cor Maria retreat center in Sag Harbor, where she had a remaining commitment, would understand if a problem developed. The director, Ann Marino, was a close friend and many of the women who attended were friends from Montauk. I quoted Rilke: "If tigers come into the temple, make that part of the ritual." But a shift of personality had begun. She had always been self-confident, assertive, and direct. Talking in public had never been fear inducing. Over the next few years we had to have a near reversal of personalities. I had to take the lead in situations where she had always covered for my social ineptitude. She became dependent on me in ways that she had always avoided.

In the months that followed, she became very jumpy. She used to refer to having the heebie-jeebies. Her primary care physician, who was a heart specialist, could not find anything wrong. She sent Maria to a psychiatrist. He was impressed by her background and personality. His first approach was to get Maria to draw on spiritual resources. When meditation did not work, he switched to medication. He tried a series of drugs, each of which produced a bad reaction. I think each of them was an anti-depressant but depression was not her problem.

In July 2001, I went to teach in Brisbane, Australia. We had previously taught at the Australian Catholic University, and they had invited us back. They were more interested in her, but I offered to do it alone and they agreed. As the time approached, I did not want to break the long-standing commitment. I went to Brisbane and returned within a week, teaching a thirty-hour graduate course while I was there. I can still picture Maria as I was leaving her at JFK; she looked confused and frightened. She who had been breezing through airports every week for many years was concerned about finding her way out to the street. I repeatedly explained where to go to get a taxi that would take her home. I called each night from the motel in Brisbane where I stayed. We talked at great length (the motel keeper thought there must have been a mistake on the phone bill until I told him that I had in fact made those calls). She seemed calm but very lonely.

For her birthday in August, I gave her what would seem to an outsider a strange gift. I told her that I would renew my driver's license (after a forty-five-year hiatus). I would then be able to take over some of the driving if she wished me to do so. I was not sure how she would take the offer. Giving up the car keys is often one of the most difficult steps for someone in an early stage of dementia. Maria liked to drive. It was for her, as for many people, a chief sign of her independence. Since I have had a lifelong hatred of the automobile, I had been happy to reverse the usual roles in which the man is assumed to be number-one driver.

I was relieved that Maria accepted my offer enthusiastically. She did not sense any plot to take away her keys, nor at that moment did I have any plan to do so. But I sensed that it might become necessary in the not too distant future so I had better start preparing the way. She did not seem to be having problems, and she continued to do some of the driving. At the end there might have been some danger, but fortunately she never had an accident. She never lost her confidence driving, but she later enjoyed being in the passenger seat.

In August, Maria's friend Rosemary Crumlin from Melbourne, visited with us in Montauk. Maria had a great fondness for Rosemary. They met in 1985 when Maria spent six weeks teaching at the National Pastoral Institute in Melbourne, where Rosemary was the director. Through phone calls and periodic visits they kept in touch. You know someone is a good friend if she travels 10,000 miles to visit you.

Rosemary was struck by Maria's change of appearance from the previous year. She was concerned about several things Maria was doing, including driving. On two evenings, Maria had what I later came to call hallucinations. When we were sitting and talking in our apartment, Maria began to see a different person than Rosemary. Later she dismissed the moment as a curious mistake. But on another evening she had a kind of vision. Rosemary awoke to find Maria standing over her and asking, "Are you an angel?" That was a more shocking experience, not unpleasant, but definitely not a run-of-the-mill happening.

Rosemary is an unusually insightful, honest, and direct person. She took me aside and asked, "Has Maria been diagnosed yet?" I was taken aback by the question; I was still denying what was becoming obvious. I reluctantly had to admit that Rosemary was seeing the situation more clearly than I was. I appreciated her candor and concern.

The incident that pushed my thinking over the edge happened in New Hampshire later that month. We were visiting with my three sisters and my brother. Maria had the greatest affection for my siblings (and they her). She had only her brother for family and now he was gone. My family had become her family. On Saturday evening, the family sat around the dinner table, talking for hours as is our wont. Maria, however, was not in the conversation at all. I finally excused us, and we went upstairs to the bedroom.

While we were getting ready for bed she suddenly asked, "Who was the woman in the red dress?" I was flabbergasted by the question. Maria had known my sister Louise for almost forty years. Maria then proceeded to ask about each of the people at the table, every one of whom she had known well for years. At that moment what crossed my mind was the thought: At some time in the future she is probably going to ask me, "And who are you?" I was right. The "some time in the future" was exactly a year later.

Diagnosis
(October 2001 to November 2001)

At the end of the summer of 2001, it was apparent that Maria needed help, but I did not know where to turn. Then, completely out of the blue, Maria received a phone call from a psychiatrist she had seen in Boston more than twenty years ago. She had not seen her since then, but Maria tended to leave a strong impression on the people she met. Apparently without any instigation, this woman called and asked Maria how she was. Perhaps sensing a problem from something conveyed in the conversation, the woman said that if Maria ever wanted to talk to a psychiatrist she had a friend she could recommend. This psychiatrist was in the East Seventies in Manhattan, an easy trip from where we lived on East Eighth Street.

Maria took up the suggestion and made an appointment. But getting there turned out to be a problem. She was suddenly fearful and confused about using the subway. It was a simple trip as I explained over and over. She still managed to get lost on the train and confused about getting to the woman's building. The woman was very kind and much impressed by Maria; nonetheless, she did not seem to know where to begin. Maria did not see much point in what was going on, and frankly, I was frustrated, too. However, in early October the psychiatrist called me and said she was concerned that Maria had physical and mental problems that she could not treat. What she did was to get us an immediate appointment at the Neurological Institute of Columbia Presbyterian Hospital.

After meeting with a neurologist at the hospital, we went back for a whole day of testing. Maria was exhausted by a battery of psychological tests that lasted about five hours. After that day, she went for various physical tests, including an MRI of the brain. Finally, after a wait of six weeks, we were given an appointment to meet with the neurologist that we had initially seen.

Both Maria and I expressed our fear of Alzheimer's. The neurologist provided a relief by first saying that it was not Alzheimer's. She said she was fairly certain of what was the matter but one symptom was missing. She asked Maria if she had ever hallucinated. Maria told her about mistaking Rosemary for an angel. The neurologist said that confirms the diagnosis. "You have Lewy Bodies," she said. I asked how to spell the word; I didn't think I had ever encountered the term.

Actually, I had seen it before on the autopsy report of Tom Harris, Maria's brother. At that time it had not registered in my memory. My second question to the neurologist was, "What is it?" Her response was, "Do you have a computer?" When I said I did, she said, "Look it up on the Internet." To put it mildly, I was surprised by her reply. I said, "Don't you have a pamphlet or something you can tell me?" She said no, she did not. She wrote a prescription for the drug Aricept and told us to come back in six months. When we protested that that was too long, she said to come back in three months.

I left the meeting puzzled but with a ray of hope. We had a name for the disease and a possible treatment. I was unacquainted with Aricept, the standard drug for Alzheimer's. Maria was familiar with it, so she knew more than I did about what the prescription meant. Maria's concern was that she had read that Aricept is only effective for six months. That is not true, but the effectiveness of Aricept is still debatable.

When we got home I immediately went to the computer. When I called up the literature on Dementia with Lewy Bodies, the first sentence I read was, "This disease is progressive, completely destructive, and always fatal." The news did not get any better after that. I looked in vain for any glimmer of hope. The description of the disease said that people live with it an average of seven years. Averages in such a case tell you nothing about an individual. One person might live one year, another person ten or twenty years. With Maria's health record, she was not in imminent risk of death. But the prospect of living for years or decades with a destroyed mind was truly dreadful. I am sure there are worse things in the world but at that moment I could not think of anything worse than watching the person you love slowly losing her mind.

I was furious at the neurologist, much of it displaced anger. First thing Monday morning I called, hoping to learn something—anything—that would be helpful and positive. I was told that she returned phone calls only between 3 and 5 PM on Fridays. That added to my ire, but I said I would be sitting by the phone from 3 PM on Friday. Come Friday I waited until it was after five. When I called her office, I was told that she had been busy. I concluded that she did not want to talk to me. At that point I didn't want to talk to her, either. I was disgusted at her handling of the situation. On reflection, I guessed that she did not want to discuss the horror of the disease in front of Maria. But she could have taken me aside and said something human to human. She is supposedly a brilliant researcher, but her interpersonal skills left room for improvement.

Dementia with Lewy Bodies can most simply be described as a combination of Alzheimer's and Parkinson's. Maria had lately complained about stiffness in her left arm. I did not connect that to the other problem she was having but it was evidence of the "parkinsonian dimension" of the Lewy Bodies. Alzheimer's is the main form of dementia so that many people equate the two words. Lewy Bodies is the second most common form of dementia, but I found that many medical people had never heard of it.

Alzheimer's was first diagnosed in 1907 by Dr. Alois Alzheimer. For more than half a century, the disease given his name was thought to be a rare occurrence found among middle-aged people. Amazingly, no one made the connection between the senility of the elderly and this supposedly rare disease of people in their forties and fifties. Hardly any research was done until 1980, a fact that I think is one of the great tragedies of twentieth-century medicine. Lewy Bodies was not diagnosed until the 1980s, so there is even less research on it than on Alzheimer's. The treatment of Lewy Bodies is difficult because of the physical and mental dimensions. The drugs for one side of the problem can interfere with drugs for the other side. The relation of the two treatments has to be carefully calibrated.

I never told Maria the whole story of Lewy Bodies. By this time the computer was beyond her, so she had to rely on my reports. When she would ask me what I had read, I never lied to her, but I also did not share all I knew. I think she was able to maintain the fiction that Lewy Bodies was not as bad as Alzheimer's, though in fact it is worse. Whether she really believed that I do not know, but I was not about to correct her false belief.

Adjusting to the Horror
(December 2001 to August 2002)

After an initial shock, human beings have a resilient tendency to adjust to whatever the situation is. Conditions of life that a few hours, days, or months previous would have seemed intolerable can become the "normal." One has to try to live with whatever has become the day-to-day experience. There is a blessing in not having to look into the abyss at every moment of the day. There can also be a disadvantage in shortening one's perception, thinking only of managing the immediate situation. Both of us started living in what the literature would probably call "denial," but denial is not all bad (as Kubler-Ross acknowledged while placing it first in the stages of dying).

Maria sometimes would ask, "What is going to happen to me?" I would answer truthfully, "I don't know; no one knows." Both of us knew that the long-term prognosis was horrible. For the caregiver, the later stages of dementia are the worst to observe. For the patient, the earlier stages must be the worst, when one is fully aware of what is happening. For my part, I would sometimes think: This is the worst experience of my life. But then I would also think: This may be the first time in my life that I have done something really good. Hannah Arendt wrote that only really bad people have good consciences. That is, most of us most of the time live with conflicts of conscience; we constantly submit our motives and actions to re-evaluation. In this case, however, I knew exactly where I had to be, what I was called to do, and why I was doing it. Maria would sometimes ask, "Why are you doing this for me?" That question had a very simple answer: "I am doing for you exactly what I know you would do for me."

An extraordinary moment occurred in December of 2001. Maria's dearest friends invited her to a beautiful spot across from New York Harbor in Rockaway Park. I was not invited; it was a women-only event, which I fully understood. A dozen or more of her friends wished to celebrate the greatness of her life while she was still able to join in the ritual. From what I gathered later, it was an event of profound joy and sorrow. As her obituary in *Newsday* noted, not many people would have the courage to take part in what was essentially a good-bye to her life of sanity. Such an event could have been cruel, but the women knew Maria well, and the ritual supported the mix of emotions that was inevitable. Maria knew that day exactly what was at stake, but her only feeling later was gratitude for the care shown by the women. They could have waited a little longer but they wanted to be sure that Maria could fully participate in the music, prayers, and conversations of the day.

In an effort to keep things normal, I went ahead with plans to use our time-share in Aruba. We owned week one in Divi Village where we had gone many times. I thought it would be a good break from the winter cold and a way to forget for a while. The week did not go well. Maria came down ill after a few days; it was diagnosed as food poisoning. Although she was not very sick, they recommended she stay overnight in the hospital. When I left at the end of visiting hours, Maria had already made friends with the half dozen other women in the ward and they were pleased to have her with them. However, I got a call in the middle of the night that her behavior was disruptive and she was demanding to talk to me. On the phone she described terrible things happening in the hospital and claimed people were trying to harm her. She had awakened in the night, and being completely disoriented, was frightened. I tried to calm her down and told her I would get her as soon as I was allowed into the hospital.

When I arrived, I found an exasperated hospital staff and patients in the ward who were upset at her behavior. It was several hours before I could get her released from the hospital. During that time she was not making much sense. However, as soon as we left the hospital, she seemed to return to a grasp of reality. When we arrived back in New York, I set about with a more serious resolve to get some help. Her behavior in the Aruba hospital impressed upon me that her hold on reality was tenuous. I knew that the medical resources of New York City are almost unlimited. I had good health insurance from my university job. But it was a mystery to me how to start. I had the bright idea of calling the wife of one of my colleagues in the department. Cindy Hosay is a professor with a specialty in gerontology and was concerned about Maria. I knew she would at least sympathize with my plight and give me some advice, but she did better than that. She put me in touch with a social worker. What I first needed was an assessment of the situation, someone who could oversee the problem as a whole and recommend specific steps.

This social worker, Kathy, proved to be an invaluable aide. She visited the apartment every other Monday. She would not only talk over things with Maria, but she became the "gatekeeper" for other services we needed. She got us an appointment with a psychiatrist at Beth Israel Hospital who is an expert on Lewy Bodies. We began to see him on a regular basis, and I finally had some confidence that the medicines were being carefully watched. On one occasion I made a separate appointment with him and he gave me a mini-course on the drugs involved. He was candid in admitting that there were no universal protocols; he had to feel his way with each patient.

The other big move in January was dumb luck on my part. In thinking about a primary care physician for Maria, I went over to where I had found one for myself. NYU runs a health care center for students just a few blocks from us. There is a small faculty practice at this center, staffed at that time by two young women physicians. I spoke to the one who was available; she was willing to take on Maria but said that her colleague, who specialized in gerontology, was better suited for the job. I hoped that Maria would feel comfortable with this energetic young woman. Alexandra and Maria hit it off immediately, and I had no difficulty in getting Maria to leave her primary care physician.

From that point on, Alexandra watched every aspect of Maria's health. After prescribing a B12 vitamin, she called and said it would be better if Maria came in every first of the month to receive a B12 shot. Each month when we came in, Maria would get a big hug and a generous amount of time for an examination of every aspect of her health. On two occasions, Alexandra phoned on a Saturday evening to recommend a change of treatment. On one of those occasions, she tracked us down in Montauk, called the pharmacy in Montauk, which was closed, and finally found a pharmacy in East Hampton so that we could pick up the prescription first thing on Sunday morning.

One striking thing about many of the people we dealt with was they weren't just in the work for the money. Alexandra mentioned to me about six months into giving the B12 shots that she had just discovered it was not covered by insurance. She did not like to ask, but would I pay for half of the expense already incurred? I said I would gladly pay the whole bill; she should not have to subsidize the cost of Maria's treatment. Something similar happened with Kathy the social worker. She mentioned after about six months that she had not been paid yet. I was shocked, having assumed that she was receiving money from the insurance company. What really shocked me was that she would travel to the apartment, sit with Maria for an hour, and supply me with useful information—while not getting paid. We fixed it up and got the proper papers filed. Filing health care claims and following up on delays and mistakes can be almost a full-time job in itself.

With the social and medical aspects of Maria's illness being monitored by competent people, I could turn my attention to two other areas: nursing homes and legal affairs. I did not want to be suddenly forced into deciding about a nursing home in the midst of a future crisis. I wanted to get a sense of what the options were, even if all the possibilities were somewhat depressing. Maria was willing, if not enthusiastic, about taking a tour of a few nursing homes. I picked out two of the best in Manhattan. An inviting aspect was that each was within fifteen minutes of where we lived. However, both of us had bad vibes as soon as we walked into them.

I have to admit that if you are not used to nursing homes, the first impression is almost sure to be a shock. These two homes were clean, well run, and equipped with numerous services for the patients. They still felt like warehouses. A lot of effort went into putting a happy face on sad and lonely lives. There were jarring elements, such as a loud-speaker system that would drive me crazy. The first place required documented proof that we had $100,000 in ready cash. The visits were worthwhile for us and on the whole not negative. But I hesitated before arranging visits to other places.

Maria would sometimes say, "Don't put me in a nursing home." I would reply: "I am not going to put you anywhere. Whatever is decided we will decide together." I was not sure I would be able to keep that promise, but I would do so if at all possible. Some time during that year I received a message via a friend from the director of a nursing home in Brentwood, Long Island: "If ever and whenever Maria needs a nursing home, she should know that she has a place here." Nothing was more helpful to my sanity than receiving this message. I knew with Maria's history that no place would be as compatible as Brentwood. Through the next year and a half, having this available option was a great relief.

On the legal front, I gathered that I needed an eldercare lawyer, someone knowledgeable in the increasingly complex legal world of the aged, sick, and dying. My total experience with lawyers was one of making out a will in the early 1990s. I looked up eldercare lawyers on the Internet and I was faced with one thousand names in Manhattan alone. I figured my best approach was to call Maria's cousin, Michael O'Brien, a lawyer on Long Island; it was the right move. Michael was particularly devoted to Maria and proved to be extraordinarily generous with his time and help during the subsequent three years. He said he knew just the person I needed.

I thought an hour's consultation to answer my questions would be enough, but I was naive about lawyer work. It required many meetings and several months before we left with a dozen legal documents (wills, living wills, power of attorney, and health care proxies). Maria came to the first few meetings and could express her views. She did not understand much of the proceedings, but neither did I. Michael insisted on coming with us to make sure we understood all the legal talk (he would not hear of taking money for all the time he put in).

I was trying to avoid having Medicaid take over my life (sixty percent of people in nursing homes are on Medicaid). Of course, at the current New York area average price of $10,000 per month, everybody except the very rich eventually runs out of money. One of the first things the lawyer recommended was that I should get maximum coverage of long-term care insurance for myself (at the time we each had modest policies). I was surprised I could get it at my age, but if you look at nursing homes you can see that not much insurance money is being paid out for men. The coverage for me was to protect her in case I went into a nursing home first. That did not seem implausible to me. At that time, I thought it was still likely that she would outlive me.

In Spring of 2002, I considered quitting my job. Maria did not want me to do that and frankly neither did I. If I were to quit work, I would have more time to attend to her, but I feared that the world would close in on us. Having a job gave me perspective and periodic relief. Of course, I could not have kept most jobs but being a university professor has its advantages. My office and classrooms are about a three-minute walk. I could still leave her alone for two hours at a time. She came to some of the classes, not as visiting teacher but as interested student.

An incident in April pointed to the difficulties of her traveling alone. I had gone to Montauk on the train; she was to follow on the bus. When the bus came in and she was not on it, I panicked. I got no answer when I called New York. I pictured her lying unconscious in the apartment or wandering the streets of Manhattan. Without thinking to leave a note, I took the next bus back to New York. Her bus had been delayed and detoured. When she arrived and I was not there, she immediately called the police to report a missing person. Two cops from East Hampton took the information and calmed her down somewhat. As soon as I entered the apartment in New York, I had a call from the police. The message: Your wife is looking for you. My department at NYU was curious as to why the East Hampton police were looking for me!

The next week I got two cell phones so that nothing similar would happen again. However, Maria was intimidated by anything technological and never became adjusted to the cell phone. I would show her repeatedly that she could reach me and some of her friends by pushing one button on the speed dial. It was still too complicated.

The part of the brain that handles even pushing one button was no longer working.

In July of 2002, I went to Norway for the ISREV conference. I would be gone for just a week, and Maria's longest and closest friend, Joanmarie Smith (a.k.a. Dulcie), came to Montauk to stay the week with her. Dulcie and she had a history of fifty years; Dulcie could do things with her that I could not. Although Dulcie has lived in Ohio for more than twenty years, she and Maria remained as close as ever, talking on the phone almost daily. I had no misgivings leaving Maria with her dearest friend who could handle whatever came up. I called each day from Norway and found Maria to be lively and enthusiastic. The only peculiarity was that she kept referring to the nuns taking care of her and the two Dulcies who were there. That seemed like a minor slip of the tongue but it presaged another stage of development and a confusion about me.

A Turn for the Worse
(August 2002 to December 2002)

One of my most vivid memories is of a Sunday evening in late August. We had been watching the last round of the PGA tourney. Suddenly, with no provocation, Maria did not know who I was. I must have reacted strongly and tried to argue with her. That made things much worse. She said she wanted to leave and go home; I insisted she could not leave and that she was already home. At one point I called Dulcie in Ohio to see if she could talk her through this confusion. That helped a little, but she still wanted to leave. When I would not let her, she asked me why I was keeping her prisoner. It got so bad that she asked me if I was going to kill her. I don't know how we got through the night. I was hopeful that by the next morning she would have forgotten the whole incident.

Although she was calm in the morning, she still did not know who I was. The mother of a close friend had died that weekend, so we went to the wake on Staten Island. On the ferryboat, at dinner, and in the funeral home, she still did not know who I was. I said to my friend, "Something seems to have snapped; I think I have lost her." On the cab ride back home, she said it was amusing that all the people there thought I was Gabriel Moran. I suggested to her that perhaps they were right but that did nothing to convince her. The confusion continued until Wednesday when I went back to Staten Island for the funeral; she preferred to stay home. When the funeral took longer than I had anticipated, I called to let her know I would be late. She recognized my voice on the phone and said excitedly, "Where have you been for the last four days? I have been looking for you." The recognition carried through when I arrived in person.

That was the first of numerous occasions when I had to cope with her confusion about who I was. When I had first heard that hallucination was part of the disease, I assumed that I could be her bridge to reality. Instead, I was what she hallucinated about. The psychiatrist said it was fairly common, a form of hallucination called Areduplication. It is directed at the people who are closest. Only with me and Dulcie did this confusion seem to occur. Maria could recognize by name people she had not seen in twenty years. But sometimes in the blink of an eye she could not recognize me.

The fortunate thing was that she usually got along with all of us. After the first incident, I learned how to react and simply go with wherever she seemed to be. Neither reasoning nor facts made any penetration once she became convinced I was another person. The metaphysics of the brain constantly surprised me. We would seem to be having an ordinary conversation, and she would suddenly ask, "You never married did you?" I would calmly answer, "Yes, I did; I married you at the NYU Catholic Center." She would just smile and listen, wondering perhaps at my confusion. Once she asked me at breakfast where I had slept the night before. When I said in the bed next to her, she said, "There were three of us in the bed!" I assured her that there were just two of us.

At times, she almost seemed to be on the inside of a playful joke. She told the psychiatrist that she could not use the toilet when she wanted because we had a public bathroom that she shared with ten men. I hastened to tell the psychiatrist that was not the case. In subsequent visits, he would ask her how many men she was now living with. With seeming playfulness, she would say four or three. I had several names; her favorite was one that went through a couple of evolutions before ending as "Bonaventura." She always got along well with kindly Bonaventura. I sometimes had the feeling that she was seeing a younger version of myself, someone she knew from thirty-five years ago. She told me one day about a nice young man who had taken her to the subway. When I told her that I was the one who had accompanied her, she said, "Oh, no; he was a young man."

One day she said to me, "How do you know I have this disease?" I replied, "I was with you when we received the diagnosis." She said, "No you weren't; I went with my mother." My instinct was to correct her and say, "Don't be foolish; your mother has been dead for ten years." Such a response would have caused her great sorrow. It might be like hearing the news of her mother's death for the first time. Like others confronted by a person living in another time zone, I learned never to force my world on hers, wherever in the past she was.

Only on a few occasions did her confusion become a situation difficult to manage in public. It took me a while to recognize that travel often brought about the confusion; the psychiatrist recommended that we not go out to Montauk. What Maria needed was stability and a consistent environment. Although our house in Montauk was a place where she was at home, the travel to there caused confusion. Once on the bus she became extremely agitated because she had left her husband behind. Why had I rushed her on to the bus without waiting for him? I had to physically restrain her from getting off the bus in Southampton. She wanted to ask if anyone had seen her husband. A few minutes later when the bus ride continued, she went to the toilet at the back of the bus; on returning to her seat she recognized the back of my head. Where had I been, she wanted to know. All my talking to her had brought no conviction at all; one glance at the back of my head did the trick.

A particularly difficult incident happened in a hotel in Philadelphia. Maria had been active in a professional organization called the Association of Professors and Researchers in Religious Education. The meeting that year, being an easy ninety-minute train ride from New York, I suggested we go. Maria was happy to do so. I knew that the women in the group would be glad to see her and would give her affirmation. They did so beyond my expectation. The difficult part came in trying to check into the hotel. After the pleasant train ride, she suddenly did not know who I was during the five-minute cab ride to the hotel. She refused to take a room with anybody except her husband. I was lost as to what to do. She finally relented enough to wait in the room until her husband arrived. Then she recognized me when I was speaking at the front of the hall and she was in the audience.

One of my most painful memories relates to Thanksgiving that year. My two sisters brought a complete turkey dinner with them down to Montauk. We had a wonderful meal and lively conversation. But after the meal, Maria took my sister Dotty aside and said, "Can you get a message to my husband; I don't think he loves me anymore, and he seems to have abandoned me." Such moments were paralyzing for me. They were indicative of great suffering on her part. I was in some sense the cause of the suffering, but I was utterly helpless to relieve it. The only recourse was patient waiting. By the next day, she might have forgotten that she had said that. For me, life became unending surprises and constant learning of how to respond to whatever might suddenly be the reality.

The Year of Living Dangerously
(January 2003 to December 2003)

When I reflect back on the year 2003, I am most struck by the many possibilities for disaster that we avoided. What I feared was that Maria would have a crippling accident. As any parent or a caregiver of a disabled person knows, one has to balance control and freedom. I did not want to hover over her every move, but that meant allowing that something untoward might happen. Many Alzheimer's patients fall and break a bone, spend time in a hospital, and then are sent for rehab to whatever nursing home is available. The family's choice is limited once this process has begun. I was determined not to follow that route.

We were still able to go out to a movie or a restaurant. In January we went to a theater up on Broadway. I had an attack of vertigo coming out of the theater. I have no idea how we got home because I could not keep the pavement from moving under my feet, and I was violently sick to my stomach. I had to lean on her to help me get home. We must have been a pretty picture making our way down those ten blocks of Broadway. But similar to what happened in June that year when I got seasick coming back from Block Island, Maria's instincts for taking care of me shifted back into operation.

I realize now that I was taking chances because I was lulled by what seemed to be normal behavior most of the time. The drugs she was taking were apparently successful in stabilizing the situation. That is, the decline was very gradual until the end of 2003. The danger in being so close to the situation is that one does not see—perhaps does not want to see—the small changes and the imperceptible descent that is occurring daily. Managing the drugs was a major task. From the start I had to watch over the ingestion of every pill she took, but that was just part of the daily routine.

A bigger problem was the apartment's layout and location. We were living just off a street bustling with buses, cars, and crowds of people. The building was constructed in the 1840s. Some aspects of the apartment were very appealing (the high ceilings, the thick walls). But the major problems were the lack of an elevator and the design of the bathroom. I was constantly warned about the stairs, that as her condition worsened she was liable to fall. Remarkably, she never had the least problem or even hesitation with the stairs right up to the end.

The bathroom was another story. Without going into all the details, suffice it to say that eventually life revolves around the bathroom. I asked the contractor for the building if he could build in guard rails. He thought it would require smashing down the wall into the next apartment. He was reluctant to do anything for which he might be legally responsible if a fall occurred. I eventually fashioned my own safety devices, learning as I went along. At present, sixty percent of Alzheimer's patients are being cared for at home. In most cases, a man is being cared for by his wife. I cannot imagine how they manage the physical part. Maria was barely a hundred pounds but I was often at my limit in trying to move her about. I also have increased respect for the twenty thousand home healthcare workers in New York City. They are not paid much more than the minimum wage for work that is both physically demanding and mentally exhausting.

By 2003, it was apparent I could no longer leave Maria for the two hours I was in class. Kathy the social worker, investigated the visiting nurse organizations in mid-town Manhattan. None could provide the flexibility I was looking for. Kathy put up a notice in St. Francis Xavier Church asking for help. That turned up a person perfect for what I needed. Delores was a retired woman who lived a few blocks away. She was the kind of help that no amount of money can buy. She was willing to come for whatever hours were needed. She and Maria immediately struck up a friendship and Maria felt completely at home with her. The two of them would sit quietly listening to music. Or they would go to Delores's apartment to visit with the two new dogs she had. It was great companionship, neither more nor less than that.

I had to make sure that Delores did not leave before I got back, especially if it was in the evening. A couple of times when I was delayed a few minutes, Maria was getting ready to go out looking for me. Fortunately, she was stopped each time by women in the building who waited with her.

One of my most frightening moments occurred in the middle of a Monday afternoon. We had hired a cleaning woman to come in every other Monday. I thought it was safe to leave Maria because she had company. When I came back from school, Maria was not there. The cleaning woman was not at fault; I had not given her any warning or instructions. Given the amount and pace of traffic right outside the door, I was fearful of her being on the street.

I rushed up and down all the streets of the neighborhood but found no trace of her. I went over to the health center, thinking that was one place she might have headed for. Actually, that was where she was, but I looked only in the waiting room and Alexandra had taken her inside. I went back to the apartment not knowing what to do next, but she showed up just a few minutes after me. She was not upset in the least; she simply thought she was keeping an appointment. I was relieved that she could find her way over to the health center on Broadway and return to the apartment. I also felt guilty for neglecting to get an ID bracelet that many Alzheimer's patients wear.

The most remarkable thing Maria did that year was to take four trips to Delaware, Ohio, to visit with Dulcie. Both Dulcie and I were amazed at her willingness to make the trip the first time and then casually to repeat it. We used the same flights on the same airline for stability sake. I would bring her to the door of the plane at LaGuardia and Dulcie would meet her at the door in Columbus. The airline people on board never had any problem. And I discovered that the airlines are very ready to provide wheelchair assistance. Just once when they did not have enough wheel chairs at the door, she took off on her own, and I found her making her way through the labyrinths of LaGuardia Airport.

Maria and Dulcie would not do much except sit and talk; they could do that endlessly. Maria was content to go each time and content to return. I realized on the last trip that I should have got on the plane with her and that I could not let her go alone again. But another trip was never possible. Making those trips must have included some shaky moments for her, especially the ninety minutes in the air. Nevertheless, I think the travel gave her a boost and released some of the spunky self-confidence she had possessed when healthy.

The other big help to me during that year was that my sister Mary took the train down from New Hampshire five times to stay with Maria over a weekend; I went out to Montauk and slept. Mary had headed an order of sisters for many years and is comfortable among the sick and aged. She is an unusually patient, kind, and understanding person. Not surprisingly, she and Maria became good friends. In addition to Dulcie, my sister was the only person I was confident could handle the situation. To stay with Maria for a couple of days was to ask too much from most people. My sister managed effortlessly, and Maria loved having her company.

There was more to do in New York City than in Delaware, Ohio, so the two of them did a little exploring. Maria insisted each time that they have a pedicure from the Korean salon next door; Maria had the idea that a pedicure had roots in the New Testament. I think a pedicure was about the last thing my sister would have got for herself but she always graciously accepted Maria's gift. And occasionally Maria could still assert her native know how. Once they went downtown to visit the World Trade Center site, an area that was still a traffic muddle. When my sister asked a cop where they could get a cab, the cop said they would have to walk several blocks north. But when my sister and the cop turned around, Maria was in the middle of the street with a cab she had just hailed.

In the fall of 2003, Cindy Hosay, who had been helpful in getting me started, gave me the name of a music therapist on the Upper East Side. The woman and her husband do wonderful work with people who are disabled, including people with dementia. Maria, as I noted earlier, was a musician, an expert pianist and singer. I had often read that music is one of the last things to go in people suffering from dementia. I thought that music therapy would be especially appropriate in Maria's case; and it was.

I bought a keyboard so that she could play at home. In my zeal to get the best instrument, I bought a keyboard that was technologically intimidating for her. When she was later in the nursing home, I bought a much simpler version of the instrument, which is where I should have started.

The therapist, Helene, was almost infinitely patient in trying to get her to perform some simple exercises. I used to sit watching for the hour and I learned lessons about teaching. Maria struggled with any kind of sequence or simple pattern. On the other hand, she could run through a tune from *Oklahoma* or a Latin hymn from her childhood. Helene was startled by Maria's ability to play a whole song from memory. One of the marvelous things about this teacher was that she would simply take her lead from the student, a trait especially important when dealing with dementia. Maria's ability to play from memory as she had all her life did not surprise me much. As with other things, but especially with music, the loss of short-term memory can leave parts of long-term memory intact.

We have learning from research that the plaque in the brain destroys specific functions and activities. People who have no short-term memory may appear stupid but they are not. They can still have a deep appreciation of the arts. The *New York Times* recently had a story in the Sunday Arts section on Alzheimer's patients. It referred to a program at a local museum for these patients. The writer seemed completely mystified by their obvious capacity for art appreciation. It is not such a surprising phenomenon; another part of the brain continues to work well despite the loss of some functions.

During 2003, Kathy got me in touch with an adult day care center in the West Village. She did some work there and promised me that it was a good place for Maria to go. Maria and I went together the first time and she agreed to go back on each Wednesday. A car would pick her up at the door in the morning and return her in the afternoon; they would call ahead to check that I was at home. A varied program of music, art, and physical therapy was provided by a staff who could not have been more cordial and hard-working. They loved having Maria because, despite her illness, she was bright and relatively active. For example, she made friends immediately with a young man who had suffered a severe stroke and could not speak. I felt awkward in his presence and did not know how to communicate with him. I don't think Maria found it to be a problem; she was her usual self and brought him out of himself.

I was hoping that she would like going to the Center. I thought it was good for her to get out of the apartment and engage in activities that I could not provide. And, frankly, it was a relief for me each Wednesday. But she soon became resistant to going; she continued to attend but with reluctance. It had nothing to do with the treatment by the staff; to a person, each of them was wonderful with her. I guessed that the reluctance stemmed from the vision that she was getting of what lay ahead for her. Many of the people who came to the center were at an advanced stage of dementia. Maria was not there yet. But I think that toward the end of 2003 she had begun to sense that the future was closing in on her.

The Year of Living Inside
(January 2004 to December 2004)

Although the drugs had seemed to work fairly well for almost two years, they suddenly seemed to be ineffective toward the end of 2003. I realize there may have been other factors at work that brought about the change. In any case, I—even I—noticed a sharp change for the worse in Maria's behavior. Both on the physical and the mental sides there were serious changes that made living in the apartment dangerous. I had assumed that my next step was going to be home nursing help around the clock. But I started to wonder if even that would be adequate for the developing situation.

I arranged for a visit during the first week in January to the nursing home in Brentwood, which is called Maria Regina Residence. We went out on the train and were given a tour of the place. Maria had lived on the property for two years when she was a novice; she had also taught there and visited many times. Her mother had even gone to school there almost a century ago. It was a place Maria was very comfortable with, and many people in the facility, both staff and residents, knew her. We were therefore received with warm friendliness. The attitude in the place was open, efficient, and compassionate. The best thing was that we both had the same impression.

At breakfast the next morning, Maria's first statement was: "It is not a question of if but when." I was surprised at her succinct statement of where we were. Nothing she could have said would have provided greater relief for me. She was taking away the burden I would have felt if I had to try persuading her that going there was in her best interest. We discussed our feeling about the place, which was very different from our reactions to the other nursing homes we had visited. We did not decide about time; I hoped to maintain my promise to do whatever was necessary when the time arose.

The director of the nursing home, Helen Clancy, called me the next day. I think she had seen something that I could not see at that time. She asked if Maria was planning to come at the beginning of the next month. I said, "Oh, no. I was thinking about the future, maybe six months or a year from now." In the course of that month, however, I came to grasp that the situation was fast becoming intolerable. I don't know if the change for the worse was precipitated by the prospect of going to the nursing home. Maria did tell my sister—but not me—that she knew she should be in a nursing home because the burden was too great on me.

An incident at the end of the month sealed my decision to move more quickly than I had thought just weeks previously. We went out for a walk in the neighborhood and everything seemed peaceful and normal. But on the way back she suddenly darted into the building next door. When I tried to get her out, she started screaming that I was attacking her. Fortunately, the super and the janitor arrived and they immediately recognized the situation. Maria trusted the janitor who offered to take her home. She kept screaming to keep me away from her.

When she had been taken back to the apartment, I sat outside on the steps waiting for her to cool down. But she came out and walked up the stairs without saying anything to me. I figured she was safe up there and would eventually have to come down. But she knocked on a door and the woman took her in. Not knowing what to do, the woman called the police. The ID Maria was carrying gave Montauk as her address. When I saw two New York City cops go by me, I suspected what they were there for. When one of them came out of the woman's apartment on the third floor, I told him that Maria lived on the next floor down.

The policemen could not have been kinder both to her and to me. They spent about twenty minutes coaxing her back to the apartment, getting her a glass of water, and making sure she was safe and calm. After I sat outside for an hour or more, I went into the apartment and she did not give the impression that anything unusual had happened. The incident is the kind of thing that caregivers regularly confront. I was lucky that things did not turn out worse. I could have been taken in by the police for questioning; that would not have been unreasonable. She could have suffered serious injury. I concluded that the "when" had now arrived.

I arranged for an entry date at the nursing home. Michael O'Brien and his brother Kevin insisted on driving us out and they stayed until we were settled. I said in Maria's eulogy that the day we arrived we were received like royalty. Not many people enter a nursing home with such an upbeat tempo. I said that the sign on her door which read, "Welcome to Maria Regina," could be read in two ways: Welcome to the place whose name is Maria Regina; or Welcome to the woman named Maria who will be treated royally.

On that day and in the year that followed she was given the best care possible. I cannot express how grateful I am for how she was treated. The staff listened to my suggestions, such as giving her the pills with yogurt rather than applesauce, or giving her regular massages of her neck and back. I was allowed to brighten her room with some of her favorite art pieces, to bring a CD player, and hook up a telephone-recording device. Many people phoned her (Dulcie almost every day). Surprisingly, she was able to function on the phone even when she was barely able to communicate in person. On the last day of her life, as her consciousness ebbed, I was convinced she recognized Rosemary's voice when she called from Melbourne.

For a good while Maria managed to remember most of the faces and names of people who visited. She had a steady stream of visitors; Michael O'Brien came faithfully every week. The one drawback with the nursing home was that Brentwood is in the middle of the traveling distance between Montauk and New York. I had to allow about four hours round trip either driving from Montauk or taking the train from New York. However, in some ways I now had more time even if I spent eight or ten hours in visiting her.

I considered getting an apartment in Brentwood but I decided that the train from New York would be less disruptive of the job I was trying to keep. I had some regrets later that I did not move. When she could not feed herself, I would have liked to be there every day at noon instead of every other day. Helping a person to eat takes time and attentiveness. When she was in the hospital, one of the staff asked me how I got her to eat whereas they could not. I said, "Well, the first thing is it takes at least half an hour." Hospitals, rehab centers, and nursing homes do not have the personnel to spend that much time with individual patients.

Until July, Maria could manage her own eating and had a healthy appetite. I had looked forward to the spring and summer when she could get out on the extensive grounds, even though by late spring she was confined to a wheelchair. One pleasant aspect of each day was going down to the chapel at 11:20 AM for the Eucharist and then going to the dining room for a leisurely dinner. I went to church more often than I had in years. It was a restful and comforting experience.

With many people in wheel chairs or struggling with various ailments, the liturgical ritual of the Catholic Mass provided a community bond. I felt that as Maria withdrew from this world, she was often praying and in touch with another dimension of reality.

The physical therapists were wonderful with her, as were the woman who did her hair and the woman who did her nails. Such small touches brightened the environment. The woman who directed the second floor's operation was a model of efficiency and kindness. I got to know the place pretty well from sitting for many hours watching the nurses, the aides, and the people who cleaned. Most of us most of the time can shut out awareness of the inner workings of nursing homes, but the work there requires patience, skill, and dedication. The pay will never be consonant with the importance of the work for an increasing part of the population.

When I had previously been in nursing homes, I was ready to climb the walls after thirty minutes. Here I was surprised that I did not find the hours to be a drag. I found I could sit in silence for long periods. Of course, I was always aware of my situation in relation to hers. I could not imagine how she passed the time. She could not read or did not wish to read (she who used to grab the crossword in the *Times* every morning). Even television—the pacifier of babies and the aged—did not interest her. I tried various things but a set of videotapes of her favorite program, "As Time Goes By," was one of my few successes.

Throughout her illness and during the time in the nursing home, Maria showed little anger. One of the best chapters in *On Death and Dying* is the chapter on anger, which warns caregivers to expect anger and not to take it personally. I sometimes thought that she (and I) might feel better if she screamed and threw things. She remained remarkably calm under almost all circumstances. When she went to a hospital or clinic for a treatment, it involved being lifted up, pushed around, strapped down, bumpily transported, but she remained serene. I, not she, would get furious when she was left on a stretcher for an hour or more in a waiting room. Her unlined face retained a strange beauty despite all she suffered. Some friends who dropped in told another friend that what struck them when they walked into the room was how beautiful she looked. It was therefore not mere blindness or bias on my part that she looked as beautiful at the end as she did the day we first met.

In October I received a call from a surgeon asking for my agreement that she have surgery for a pressure sore. The sore, which had been there from before she entered Maria Regina, was not responding to treatment. The surgeon said it was necessary to operate; otherwise, "it could mean her demise." I obviously had to agree to the surgery. Until that time, I still did not understand the seriousness of a pressure sore; I thought it was just a bother and an irritation. When Christopher Reeve died that month, the press carried stories that most people with dementia die from pressure sores that become infected.

I was told that she would be in the hospital for seven days and in rehab for fourteen days. What happened was that she was in each place for about seven weeks. Neither place was bad, but they were not as comfortable as the nursing home. I used to say that one's expectations have been shortened when all one hopes for is to get well enough to go to the nursing home. After she was many weeks in the hospital, a surgeon said to me, "We want to get her out of here because the longer you stay in a hospital the more problems you develop." I thought that was surprising if somewhat depressing candor about hospitals.

When it came time to move, I had a choice among a few rehab centers that had the proper machine to help her healing. My best choice was a place in East Patchogue, Long Island, which added a few more hours to my travel but which seemed a decent place. But after almost two months of treatment in the rehab center, she showed little progress. I did not think it was anyone's fault; they did what they could. I was asked to agree to insertion of a feeding tube—a temporary tube—to improve nutrition. I would not have agreed to a permanent tube but after a while temporary tends toward permanent. At one point I looked at her with five different lines running into her body. I had approved each thing separately but I began to wonder if the total result was just a form of torture.

The house physician was a nice enough man but not much involved with her case. When I asked him in early December when she might be able to leave, he replied quite casually, "Oh, I don't think she will ever leave." His candor shook me up. Until then I was concentrating on each day while I waited for the rehab to be over. His remark forced me to start considering that if the wound from the surgery had not healed, the end might be near. My sisters had seen this in October when they visited Maria in the hospital, but for me it was a sudden awakening in December.

The Final Goodbye
(December 2004 to February 2005)

On Christmas day of 2004, I knew that Maria was dying. I had gone out to the rehab center with Dulcie and Elaine Roulet, another close friend of Maria's. This pair with their outgoing friendliness brought cheer to any room they entered. I knew that if they could not get a rise out of her, then she had passed a point of no return. When we entered the room, Maria closed her eyes. Whether the movement was voluntary or not, it was shockingly different from the past, even a few weeks earlier, when the three of us visited her in the hospital. We shared Christmas day with her but with little response on her side.

I talked to the house physician again. He knew a little more about her case now. His prognosis was more guarded but no more optimistic. I asked him if he had communicated information to her primary-care physician, but I found that he did not know who that was. I offered him the phone number so he could call. I must admit I was still naive about the communication of information among healthcare providers. It finally came home to me two weeks later when I asked one of the surgeons about the antibiotics Maria had been taking. The surgeon had no knowledge of that. When I gave the name of the person who prescribed the drugs to the rehab center they did not recognize the name. The light finally dawned: I was the only person who actually was aware of all the parties involved. Unless I functioned as the link, these people did not talk to each other.

The next week her primary-care physician called. Dr. Ryan Cahill was a fine, caring physician serving the nursing home. He had always been straightforward with me, doing what he could for her but honest about the limitations of any treatment. I asked what he thought and he replied, "Tell me what you want and then I will tell you what I think." Not many physicians are that willing to listen. I said that the wound had not healed. One choice was to go back into the hospital for more surgery but that was unlikely to succeed. More surgery and antibiotics would probably just add to her discomfort. However, without further surgery she was likely to develop an infection. He agreed.

Then I asked him to describe to me what it is like to die of sepsis or septic shock—which he did. He assured me that pain could be completely controlled. We agreed that she should return to the nursing home and be given palliative care. Good Shepherd Hospice was contacted to give us additional help in keeping her comfortable.

When Maria returned from the hospital to the nursing home she was given a quiet room on the first floor with ready access to any service she might need. Staff from the second floor where she had previously been came down to see her.

She stopped receiving nutrition because her body could no longer tolerate it. There are acrimonious debates in this country that surround "the removal of the feeding tube." The tube is not actually removed; nutrition is simply halted. Some people scream murder when there is such a move; they claim the patient has been starved to death. There are some debatable cases, but most of the time the inability to take food is a sign that the body is preparing for death. In any case, the cause of death is not "starvation," an inappropriate name for allowing the person to die. In Maria's case, continuing the feeding would have worsened her condition because the body could not absorb the nutrition.

When I arrived on Saturday, January 29, the nurse told me that Maria probably had only a few days to live. Obviously, I should have known the end was coming soon, but it still caught me by surprise that it would be so quick. I moved into the nursing home, staying in a guest room that they had provided whenever I wished to stay overnight. My sister and brother-in-law came down from New Hampshire and the three of us went to the funeral home to make arrangements. Afterwards, I would be relieved that all of that preparation was in place.

On the morning of February 1, I was waiting for Dr. Cahill. When he arrived and I asked him what he thought, he replied, "You have been here more than anyone; you tell me." I was again surprised by his willingness to listen, rather than play the expert. After he heard what I had seen in the past few days, he checked her chart. When he saw that her kidneys were essentially closed down, he said she could not last long. I stayed with her throughout the day trying to aid her breathing. Her lungs were filling with fluid. Listening to a person dying of pneumonia is disconcerting. There is obvious discomfort for the patient that cannot be removed but no apparent pain. I went out briefly for dinner and when I came back her breathing was more labored. I did not recognize the gurgling of a dying person. A nun who had great affection for Maria stayed with us. She recognized better than I how close death was. She had seen it dozens of times; I had little experience.

I held Maria and tried to keep her mouth clear, but, of course, my efforts were futile. When the staff tried to suction the lungs, I thought for a moment that her breathing had suddenly improved and then I realized that she had stopped breathing. The time was 9:50 PM; the last moments had been relatively peaceful. Two other nuns came in to pray and to provide immediate assistance. I called my sister and her husband who had gone over to their motel a few hours previous. They immediately returned and stayed with me until the funeral home came for the body.

Immediate Aftermath
(February 2005)

The next day I was mostly in a daze. Most of the funeral arrangements had been made, and I had plenty of help in attending to whatever had to be done immediately. By the middle of the day, there was nothing more for me to do in the nursing home so I went into New York. I was waiting for a call from the funeral home, which was trying to arrange an autopsy. Michael O'Brien had asked me if I would have an autopsy, concerned about the presence of Lewy Bodies in the family gene pool.

The funeral home had difficulty finding an available pathologist. Rather than sit alone in my apartment, I went over to school and met my graduate course. I could have canceled the class; the students were probably surprised that I came. I did not think of it as heroism. I simply found that teaching that day and throughout the semester was therapeutic for me. The students were wonderfully supportive and it gave me a chance to talk out my feelings. At about 10 PM that evening, I got a call from a pathologist. She said she was willing to perform the autopsy the next morning. However, she needed a check for $4000 dollars before she would begin. Early next morning I was on the Long Island Railroad, check in hand.

The delay for the autopsy pushed back the wake until the weekend and the burial until Monday. That schedule was probably a fortunate one because it gave time for people to read the notice in the papers and to travel from great distances. The day before her death, I had written several obituaries. The first obituary was for the *New York Times*. I knew that it was a long shot getting a story into the *Times*. Our wedding had gotten a write up, but that was when Tom Harris was with the paper. As it turned out, I gladly paid for the notice in the *Times* that would be read by many people in New York and beyond. In the second case, *Newsday* did not use the obituary that I had written for them but they assigned a staff person to write the story. They had a fine picture taken on our deck in Montauk when they had done a feature on Maria. I was delighted with the picture and story they ran.

I knew that most people coming to the wake would be expecting the standard Irish Catholic format. If the choice were just for myself, I would not have gone along with an open casket and many other features. I allowed the body to be embalmed though I consider the practice to be weird. A steady stream of people came for the two days. I met some people that I had not seen in twenty, thirty, or forty years.

I had chosen a church for the funeral as a result of a helpful suggestion by Padraic O'Hare. The pastor in this church, John Rowan, not only knew Maria but also was amenable to having what we wished for the burial service. I went over to the church with Dulcie and my sister Mary to talk with the liturgist about music, prayers, and the rest of the ceremony. Elaine, the parish liturgist, had a more coherent picture of how to handle things than any of the three of us. Thus, the funeral was done with a beautiful simplicity in elegant surroundings. It included music Maria would have loved. The pastor spoke with warmth about Maria. I provided the eulogy toward the end of the service. I concluded the eulogy with an Irish prayer that Maria had spoken at her mother's funeral.

Maria had given me instructions about burial in a plot next to her father and mother. That required a long funeral procession from Sayville, Long Island, to Middle Village, Queens. At the gravesite, Padraic delivered the final poetic testimony. Then fifty of us went for a meal at a nearby restaurant. Michael O'Brien had efficiently arranged that part of the day. The food, drink, laughter, and tears flowed in abundance. Maria would have loved it, her kind of gathering.

Maria's story comes to its essential close with the funeral; this memoir is her story, not mine. I will add only some details about a few public forums of mourning by her friends immediately afterward. I estimate that I received about four hundred letters of condolence. Some of them were e-mails that could be answered briefly. But most were lengthy handwritten letters. If anyone had told me a year ago that I would be faced with answering four hundred letters, I would have said I could not do it. Strangely, I did not find writing replies to be burdensome. Writing a brief note of thanks to people who expressed their deep-felt sorrow was therapeutic.

The range of letters was remarkable from people who knew her since childhood to a priest who had visited her classroom for an hour in 1962 and never forgot her. I was particularly struck by a number of gay/lesbian former students for whom Maria was their chief support when homosexuality was not an open issue. I am sure she never thought of gay rights as a cause. It simply wasn't in her nature to discriminate against "outsiders." She often described herself as an outsider in institutions where she worked. That seemed odd, given that she seemed so easily accepted wherever she went. But I think she never forgot the feeling she had as an eight year old who was hustled off to the playground and not told that her father had just dropped dead. She seemed to have an instant rapport with people who are considered by society to be of low status. I used to sit back and marvel at this talent for talking to anybody.

Through the effort of Professor John Hull in England, ISREV established a Web site. Members were invited to submit testimonies about Maria. Many of the group had already written to me. John Hull collected about two dozen of these remembrances and posted them along with a small selection of photos. Unfortunately, the digital camera had not come into general use before Maria's sickness so photos are not as easily and clearly transferred to the Internet. I used to kid her that the best picture she ever took was one taken while she was on a white water raft on the Colorado River. Since she was holding on for her life, she was not posing for the camera. The result is a picture with all the wonderful emotions of her inner life evident on her face.

Two gatherings shortly after Maria's death stand out in my mind. Fordham University's religious education department organized a memorial on March 22. Professor Gloria Durka, the most steadfast friend one can imagine, organized the program along with her colleague Kieran Scott. Kieran delivered a beautiful tribute to Maria, based on thirty-five years of friendship with Maria and myself. I left for the memorial in plenty of time; the train ride from Grand Central is about twenty minutes. It is probably a reflection of my mental state at the time that I—who spends much of his life on trains—got off at the wrong stop. I showed up an hour and a half late after walking through much of the South Bronx. I felt just awful, having delayed the service and then missing most of it. Few of the current students had known Maria except through her writing. Nonetheless, her spirit was somehow present through the faculty that did know her. I should add that Fordham had not waited to pay tribute to her only after her death. They had honored her in December 2002, when she could still appreciate the praise lavished on her by faculty and students.

Just a few days after Fordham's tribute, I went down to Hollywood, Florida, at the invitation of Joseph and Mercedes Iannone. The Iannones have for decades done superb work in education first with families and parishes then at St. Thomas University in Miami. I knew that being with them would be a comfortable and comforting situation. Since Maria and I had taught at St. Thomas, many people there knew and admired her. On Sunday evening (the eve of our wedding anniversary), the Iannones got together an intimate gathering of friends who offered remembrances of Maria. What was unusual, I recognized part way into the evening, was that everyone in the gathering had recently suffered his or her own loss or death. They understood the feeling of grief. Anyone in mourning can become too self-absorbed, forgetting that the world is filled with other mourners. This simple, poignant moment in South Florida was a fitting tribute to Maria's simple joy in the small things of life. She was a dynamo of energy for good, even in her sickness, and I like to believe that her presence did not end with her death.

ENDNOTES

Introduction

p. 1. Martin Buber, *I and Thou* (New York: Scribner's, 1958), 1.

p. 1. Maxim Gorky, *Reminiscences of Tolstoy, Chekhov, and Andreev* (London: Hogarth Press, 1934), 136.

p. 1. C.S. Lewis, *A Grief Observed* (San Francisco: Harper, 2001).

p. 1. Andrew Greeley, *Religious Change in America* (Cambridge: Harvard University Press, 1996), 105.

p. 5. Gisela Webb, *Cross Currents*, Fall 2001, 324–35.

Chapter One

p. 13. *Dogmatic Constitution on the Church*, in *Documents of Vatican II* (New York: Guild Press, 1966), no. 9.

p. 13. *Constitution on the Church*, no. 14.

p. 17. Walter Brueggemann, *The Land* (Philadelphia: Fortress Press, 1977), 5.

p. 18. Poll cited in *National Directory for Catechesis* (Washington: USCCB, 2005), 27.

p. 21. John Howard Yoder, *Fullness of Christ* (Elgin: Brethren Press, 1987), 46.

p. 21. *Constitution on the Church*, no. 10.

p. 22. Brian Froehle and Mary Gauthier, eds. *Catholicism USA: A Portrait of the Catholic Church in the United States* (New York: Orbis Books, 2001), 121.

p. 22. *Declaration on Ecumenism*, no.11.

p. 23. *Constitution on the Church*, no. 7.

p. 24. *Constitution on the Church*, no. 18, 30.

p. 25. Friedrich von Hugel, quoted in Rosemary Haughton, *The Catholic Thing* (New York: Templegate, 1997), 18.

p. 27. Jaroslav Pelikan, *Vindication of Tradition* (New Haven: Yale University Press, 1986), 64.

p. 27. William Temple, *Nature, Man, and God* (New York: Macmillan, 1935), 176.

p. 28. Garry Wills, *What Jesus Meant* (New York: Viking, 2006).

p. 31. Karl Rahner, *Theological Investigations*, vol. 16 (New York: Crossroad, 1983), 219.

Chapter Two

p. 34. John Roberto, *Becoming a Church of Lifelong Learners* (New London: Twenty-Third Publications, 2006), 43.

p. 40. Bernard Bailyn, *Education in the Forming of American Society* (New York: Vintage Books, 1960).

p. 41. John Dewey, "My Pedagogic Creed," in *Dewey on Education*, Martin Dworkin, ed. (New York: Teachers College Press, 1959), 13–32.

p. 42. John Dewey, *Democracy and Education* (New York: Free Press, 1961), 76.

p. 47. John Dewey, "Religious Education as Conditioned by Modern Psychology and Pedagogy," *Religious Education* 69 (January, 1974), 5–11.

p. 47. Jean Piaget, *The Moral Judgment of the Child* (New York: Collier Books, 1962), 361.

p. 48. David Elkind, *Children and Adolescents* (New York: Oxford University Press, 1978), 99.

p. 49. Thomas Aquinas, *On Truth*, q. 11, a. 1.

p. 49. *National Directory for Catechesis*, 185.

p. 50. Jaroslav Pelikan, *Jesus through the Centuries* (New Haven: Yale University Press, 1985), 17.

p. 50. Augustine, *Against the Academicians; The Teacher* (Indianapolis: Hackett Publishing, 1995).

p. 50. Yves Congar, "A Semantic History of the Term Magisterium," in *The Magisterium and the Theologian*, Charles Curran and Richard McCormick, eds. (New York: Paulist Press, 1982), 210.

p. 51. Barbara Grizzuti Harrison, *Off Center* (New York: Dial Press, 1980), 40.

p. 52. George Elliot, *Middlemarch* (New York: Barnes and Noble, 1976), 825.

Chapter Three

p. 57. Marcus Buckingham, *The One Thing You Need to Know* (New York: Free Press, 2005), 22.

p. 59. John Dewey, *Democracy and Education* (New York: Free Press, 1916), 83.

p. 60. *National Directory for Catechesis*, 100.

p. 60. Eric Gritsch, *Martin—God's Jester: Luther in Retrospect* (Philadelphia: Fortress Press,1983), 187.

p. 60. *Constitution on the Church*, 11:5; *The Church in the Modern World*, 48:8.

p. 61. Eliot Daley, *Father Feelings* (New York: Pocket Books, 1979), 65.

p. 63. *Catechism of the Catholic Church*, no. 226.

p. 67. Robert Wuthnow, *American Mythos* (Princeton: Princeton University Press, 2006), 58.

p. 68. Kenneth Smith and Ira Zepp, *Search for the Beloved Community* (New York: Judson Press, 1998), 121.

p. 70. Edmund Morgan, *The Puritan Family* (New York: Harper and Row, 1966), 68, 76.

Chapter Four

p. 73. *Constitution on the Sacred Liturgy*, no. 14.

p. 74. Reinhold Niebuhr, *Christian Century*, December, 1984, 1197.

p. 75. *Constitution on the Sacred Liturgy*, no. 113.

p. 78. Mary Douglas, *Natural Symbols* (New York: Vintage Books, 1970), 64.

p. 78. Evagrius Ponticus, *The Praktikos* (Spenser: Cistercians, 1970), 12.

p. 79. Judith Martin, quoted in Robert Evans, *Family Matters* (San Francisco: Jossey Bass, 2004), 79.

p. 79. Eli Wiesel, *Souls on Fire* (New York: Simon and Schuster, 1982), 72.

p. 79. Tom Driver, *Patterns of Grace* (New York: Harper and Row, 1977), 131.

p. 82. Bill Huebsch, *Whole Community Catechesis in Plain English* (New London: Twenty-Third Publications, 2002), 100, appendix 5.

p. 82. Congregation for the Clergy, *General Directory for Catechesis* (Washington: USCCB, 1997), no. 71.

p. 83. Karl Barth, *Church Dogmatics*, vol 3, part 3 (Edinburgh: T&T Clark, 1969), 299.

p. 83. Catherine Madsen, *The Bones Reassemble: Reconstituting Liturgical Speech* (Aurora, CO: Davies Group, 2005), 63.

p. 84. Geoffrey Gorer, *Death, Grief, and Mourning* (Garden City: Doubleday, 1965).

p. 89. Karl Rahner, *The Practice of Faith* (London: Macmillan, 1985), 72.

p. 90. Thomas Merton, *Conjectures of a Guilty Bystander* (Garden City: Image Books, 1965), 54.

p. 90. Abraham Joshua Heschel, *The Sabbath* (New York: Farrar, Straus, and Giroux, 1951), 31.

Chapter Five

p. 95. Joseph Yerushalayim, *Zakhor* (New York: E. Even B. Ravid, 1997), 10.

p. 96. G. K. Chesterton, *Orthodoxy* (New York: Image Books, 1959), 60.

p. 96. Flannery O'Connor, *Mystery and Manners* (New York: Farrar, Straus, and Giroux, 1969), 192.

p. 97. Richard Rorty, *Essays on Heidegger and Others* (Cambridge: Cambridge University Press, 1991), 81.

p. 97. Ken Bain, *What the Best College Teachers Do* (Cambridge: Harvard University Press, 2004), 122.

p. 98. W.H. Auden, quoted in Gareth Matthews, *The Philosophy of Childhood* (Cambridge: Harvard University Press, 1998), 103.

p. 99. John Dominic Crossan, *Raid on the Articulate* (New York: Harper and Row, 1976), 178.

p. 101. Flannery O'Connor, *Wise Blood* (New York: New American Library, 1983), 60.

p. 103. Bill Huebsch, *Whole Community Catechesis in Plain English*, 36.

p. 104. Flannery O'Connor, *The Habit of Being* (New York: Farrar, Straus, and Giroux, 1979), 348.

p. 104. Mark Twain, *Hannibal Courier-Post*, March 1, 1835.

p. 105. Eli Wiesel, *Souls on Fire*, 71.

p. 105. Bill Huebsch, *Whole Community Catechesis in Plain English*, 31.

p. 105. Quoted in Robert Wilken, *John Chrysostom and the Jews* (Berkeley: University of California Press, 1983), 106.

p. 106. Franz Rosenzweig, *Star of Redemption* (Notre Dame: University of Notre Dame Press, 1985), 178.

p. 106. H. Richard Niebuhr, *The Kingdom of God in America* (New York: Harper, 1959), 106.

p. 106. Quoted in Hans Waldenfals, *Absolute Nothingness* (New York: Paulist Press, 1980), 132.

p. 107. Alasdair McIntyre, *Three Versions of Moral Enquiry* (Notre Dame: University of Notre Dame Press, 1990), 33.

p. 109. John Henry Newman, *Grammar of Assent* (Garden City: Image Books, 1955), 89.

Chapter Six

p. 111. "Yersuhalmi Sanhedrin 4:2" in *The Essential Talmud*, Adin Steinsaltz, ed. (New York: Basic Books, 1984).

p. 112. Raymond Brown, *Community of the Beloved Disciple* (New York: Paulist Press, 1978).

p. 113. Frank Tobin, *Meister Eckhart: Thought and Language* (Philadelphia: University of Pennsylvania Press, 1986), 86.

p. 114. George Lindbeck, *The Nature of Doctrine* (Louisville: Westminster John Knox, 1984), 64.

p. 114. Pope Pius XII, *The Pope Speaks* 4 (1958), 397.

p. 115. Quoted in Thomas Merton, *Conjectures of a Guilty Bystander* (1968), 129.

p. 118. Karl Rahner, *The Christian of the Future* (New York: Herder and Herder, 1967), 65.

p. 118. *National Directory for Catechesis*, 176.

p. 119. Mary Ann Glendon, *A World Made New: Eleanor Roosevelt and the Universal Declaration of Human Rights* (New York: Random House, 2002).

p. 120. Dietrich Bonhoeffer, *Ethics* (New York: Touchstone Books, 1995), 283.

p. 121. *Catechism of the Catholic Church*, no. 24.

p. 122. Horace Bushnell, *Christian Nurture* (Grand Rapids: Baker, 1979), 4.

p. 123. John Calvin, quoted in Haugaard, *Faith and Church* (Philadelphia: Fortress Press, 1988), 144.

p. 125. Paul Tillich, *Ultimate Concern* (New York: Harper, 1965), 194.

p. 126. Dietrich Bonhoeffer, *Letters and Papers from Prison* (New York: Touchstone, 1997).

Chapter Seven

p. 130. Robert Greenleaf, *Servant Leadership* (New York: Paulist Press, 2002).

p. 130. Kennan Osborne, *Order and Ministry* (New York: Orbis Books, 2006), 42.

p. 131. Albert Camus, *The Plague* (New York: Vintage Books, 1948), 119.

p. 131. Victor Frankl, *Man's Search for Meaning* (Boston: Beacon Press, 2000).

p. 131. Friedrich Nietzsche, *Genealogy of Morals* (Garden City: Doubleday, 1956).

p. 132. Simone Weil, *A Simone Weil Reader* (London: Moyer Bell, 1985), 24.

p. 135. *The Pastoral Constitution on the Church in the Modern World*, no. 1.

p. 135. *Our Hearts Were Burning Within Us* (Washington: USCCB, 1999), no. 61.

p. 136. Henry Shue, *Basic Rights* (Princeton: Princeton University Press, 1996).

p. 136. Quoted in Jim Wallis, *God's Politics* (San Francisco: Harper, 2005), 16.

p. 137. Mary Douglas, *Natural Symbols*, 40.

p. 137. P. N. Furbank, *Behalf* (Lincoln: University of Nebraska Press, 2000), 57.

p. 138. Gustavo Gutierrez, *A Theology of Liberation* (New York: Orbis Books, 1988), 174.

p. 141. Joseph Nye, *The Paradox of American Power* (New York: Oxford University Press, 2003).

p. 141. Max Weber quoted in James McGregor Burns, *Leadership* (New York: Harper and Row, 1978), 12.

p. 141. *New York Times*, February 19, 2003, 1.

p. 141. George Kennan, *New York Times*, November 18, 2005, 25.

p. 142. Reinhold Niebuhr, *Moral Man and Immoral Society* (Louisville: Westminster/John Knox, 2002); *Man's Nature and His Communities* (Washington: University Press of America, 1988).

p. 142. Max Weber, "Politics as a Vocation" in *From Max Weber: Essays in Sociology*, Hans Gerth and C. Mills Wright, eds. (New York: Oxford University Press, 1946), 77–128.

p. 142. Herbert Marcuse quoted in Pinchas Lapide, *Sermon on the Mount* (New York: Orbis Books, 1986), 96.

p. 143. Pinchas Lapide, *Sermon on the Mount*, 99.

p. 143. William James, *The Moral Equivalent of War and Other Essays* (New York: Harper and Row, 1971), 295.

p. 143. Thomas Merton, *Seeds of Destruction* (New York: Macmillan, 1964), 90.

p. 144. *The Pastoral Constitution on the Church in the Modern World*, no. 82.

p. 144. George Gallup, *The American Catholic People: Their Beliefs, Practices, and Values* (New York: Doubleday, 1987), 82.

p. 145. United States Conference of Catholic Bishops, *The Challenge of Peace: God's Promise and Our Response* (Washington: USCCB, 1983).

p. 145. George Kennan, *New York Times*, May 1, 1983, 15.

p. 145. *Economic Justice for All: A Pastoral Letter on Catholic Social Teaching and the U.S. Economy* (Washington: USCCB, 1986), no. 13.

p. 145. "American Catholics Survey," *National Catholic Reporter*, September 30, 2005.

p. 146. Jonathan Schell, *The Unconquerable Earth* (New York: Owl Books, 2004), 144.